Contents

Foreword

When I started reading Jack Miller's *Repentance*, I felt as speechless as the guy in Matthew 22 who finds himself at the wedding banquet (having somehow slipped security checkpoints) only to be escorted to the exit for want of the required garment. He should have known better; there had been announcements.

I should have known better too. A quarter century after the fanfare of a conversion experience, I realized I had become a Christian without authentic repenting. I suppose there had been announcements along the way of the need to be broken over sin. But for some of us it never ran deep. We limited ourselves "to a generalized confession of sins during worship that amounts to little more than a solemn liturgical formula. I have rarely seen anyone undergo fundamental change through it" (p. 38).

It's like Miller read my mail. And not only mine, evidently: "Much of the church resembles a desert," he writes. "Frankly, I know of very few confessing Christians who have ever shed tears over their sins. Or if once they wept over their sins, they are careful never to do it again [because] they see no one else doing it . . ." (pp. 41, 86–87).

The book's title is *Repentance*, but this is no ivory tower exercise about where repentance fits into the *ordo salutis*, whether before or after faith and regeneration. It is nothing less than an attempt to reclaim biblical Christianity from a modern powerless variety that downplays or ignores the robust repentance that was the gateway to salvation in the Great Commission (Luke 24:44–47).

Andrée Seu
Senior Writer, *WORLD Magazine*
Author of *Won't Let You Go Unless You Bless Me,*
Normal Kingdom Business and *We Shall Have Spring Again*

A Note to the Reader

MY PURPOSE in writing down these things was not to produce a book with a formal outline, but to shape the truths God has taught me into an informal essay. What you have here, then, is something of a single letter from my heart to yours. It expresses a twofold concern for God's people today. First, many who call Jesus their Savior are loaded down with pretense and evasion, and they have no heart for confessing and forsaking their ways as God commands them (Prov. 28:13, 1 John 1:8–10). Second, many others have an awareness of their guilt, but do not know how to go to Christ and rid themselves of their dark blots. In their secret heart God is viewed as an unsympathetic tyrant, not as the Father of our Lord Jesus Christ.

From my good friend Kefa Sempangi I have heard about the working out of these principles in Uganda, where a revival which began in 1938 has continued up to the present. Kefa reports that the believers there have an unusual honesty in confessing sins, and as a consequence the whole church has been filled with great joy. In practice this means that a grim-faced brother may be stopped on the street and asked by his fellow Christian, "My brother, have you confessed your sins today? Have you seen the cross of Christ today?"

According to Kefa, believers are expected to "see the cross" when they confess their sins and to leave their burdens there. My heart's desire is the same for you who read this treatise. Do not attempt to confess and forsake your old ways apart from the love of God manifested in a crucified Lord. Instead, look to the risen Savior who intercedes at the Father's right hand for you. As the Spirit exposes the evils of your heart, observe the wounds in Christ's hands. They are the absolute, unshakable promises of the Father guaranteeing full access to the crushed in spirit. Therefore, as you read, believe, and He will wash your tears in the blood of the Lamb.

Repentance: The Foundation of Life

MOST of this study on repentance I wrote at a time when God had made me aware of the greatness of His love in a new way. This new consciousness of His everlasting mercy came as I learned to confess my own sins more forthrightly and to turn from them with deeper hatred for every evil impulse in my heart. The joy and relief this gave my struggling soul is simply beyond words. At that hour something of the glory of the cross appeared before my eyes with transforming and healing power.

What we all desperately need to see is that the love of a holy God is manifested covenantally at the cross. In the sacrifice of the Lamb of God, the Father *promises* to receive contrite sinners on a daily—no, hourly—basis. The cross says, "No matter what your sins, unlimited mercy is available to those who turn to God through Jesus' merits." Thus, at Calvary we behold the infinite nearness and compassion of the infinitely majestic God. The Father, in the gift of His Son, has put Himself under eternal obligation to returning children. Having satisfied the demands of His own holy law, the Father *must* open His mighty arms and embrace every returning child. And He must do it every day. He has promised to do it (Luke 15:11–32, 1 John 1:8–10), and God cannot lie (Heb. 6:13–20).

To be near God and to have God near us is the whole purpose of human life.

But without sincere repentance there can be no face-to-face fellowship with the Father of lights.

An unrepentant heart is self-satisfied, proud and cold. God resists such a heart. Scripture says flatly, "God resists the proud" (James 4:6).

But the Lord cannot resist the broken heart that has experienced true repentance. He will not, He cannot, stay away from repentant sinners. He says, "Be zealous and repent." Then as the door of repentance is opened by His almighty grace, He comes in and eats with the contrite ones and fills them with the joys of His friendship (Rev. 3:19–20).

It is not easy for us to understand this, otherwise the Lord would not repeat it so often in the Scriptures. His Word says, "The LORD is near to those who have a broken heart" (Ps. 34:18). Awakened from his terrible lapse into carnality, David cries, "The sacrifices of God are a broken spirit. . . ." (Ps. 51:17). And the prophet Isaiah is told by the high and lofty One, "I dwell in the high and holy place, with him who has a contrite and humble spirit" (Isa. 57:15).

No sentimentalist inviting sinners to self-pity, this holy Father sees humanity in all its nastiness and is yet given to strange, tender excesses. His love explodes into joyous action whenever a convicted sinner turns toward home. A glimpse of the exile is enough. The Father quickly goes forth to receive the penitent one into His arms. What He has to give, He gives: the ring and the shoes of family relationship, the feast of heavenly joy and—best of all—Himself (Luke 15:22–24).

Yet few contemporary Christians understand the importance of repentance in the reconciliation between God and sinful humanity. Few even know that the Great Commission includes a command to preach repentance: "that repentance and remission of sins should be preached in His name to all nations, beginning at Jerusalem" (Luke 24:47). They do not share the divine excitement over repentant sinners either. If they did, they would want to enter into it. They themselves would repent, and then they would go and plead with sinners to receive the same joy. Once tasted, repentance would speak to them of communion with Christ and of self-forgetting fruitfulness and of Kingdom power (Mark 1:15).

This is the age of the Spirit, and the age of the Spirit is an epoch of repentance. This new day was introduced by the preaching of repentance by John the Baptist and Jesus (Mark 1:4, 14–15). The apostolic message to the unconverted was a testimony of "repentance toward God and faith toward our Lord Jesus Christ" (Acts 20:21). In Athens the sophisticated Greeks were told that it was a very special time in which they were living. By raising Jesus from the dead, God had served notice to all people everywhere to repent, because He had fixed a day for judging the world by this same Man (Acts 17:30–31). The Spirit had the same message for the churches of Asia Minor. "Be zealous and repent," said Christ and the Spirit (Rev. 3:19).

But most importantly, it is at Pentecost that the power of the new age descended. Here we discover that the new order did not begin with an invitation to seek the Spirit first of all. Rather, people were commanded to repent for what they had done with Jesus. Then they were assured that they too would be filled with the Spirit of promise. Peter said, "Repent, and let every one of you be baptized in the name of Jesus Christ for the remission of sins; and you shall receive the gift of the Holy Spirit" (Acts 2:38, see also 3:19–20).

We have sinned by failing to teach and practice this commandment of the King. We have become small people, the least in the Kingdom (Matt. 5:19). Satan has deceived us. By our self-trust and self-dependence, the Spirit has been so quenched that many, many churches, pastors, Christian workers and laypeople think that things are just fine, when in fact we have been visited with the dryness of death (Jer. 17:5–6, 13).

In our pride we would never think of ourselves in connection with Ananias and Sapphira. But our sin bears a very close resemblance to theirs. They wanted to pretend to be near God when they were not. In doing this they lied to the Holy Spirit by publicly claiming to have given *all* the proceeds from the sale of their property to the Lord (Acts 5:1–2). How close we are today to the inner spirit of this terrible deed! We bring a *part* of ourselves to the Lord—and not always the best part—and then we want people to think that we are near God. This is to substitute the role of a Christian for the reality. True, we can effect a certain awe in our prayers as we tell the Lord that "we are not worthy of the least of all Thy mercies." Yet such praying does not get the fountain clean at its deepest source. It says very little about particular sins which we commit daily and the root-sins of pride, un-belief and lust which clog up our lives.

The sad truth is that we are like the Pharisees who loved the *reputation* for knowing God more than they loved God. They were expert Bible students who searched the Scriptures with the conviction that they taught the way to eternal life (John 5:39). Despite the intensity of zeal which made their religion seem so authentic, Jesus said that it was all pretense. For in their hearts they were blinded because they sought glory from one another and not from God (John 5:44).

So in their pride they were not near God. Instead, they were under Satan's influence. Full of themselves and their own thoughts, they did not really seek to be taught of God (Isa. 29:11–14). Hence, they were blinded in a very deep way. They were those who saw everything so clearly without really seeing anything at all (John 9:40–41).

We are terribly foolish if we think that contemporary men and women do not see that many are putting on a false show.

The world of humanity in our generation has been domi-nated by lies, broken promises, shattered illusions and just general sham. People are sick and tired of role-players and plastic goods, slickly turned out and calculated to deceive. Therefore, if we wish to be effective, we must see that our own pharisaic pretense will eventually be discovered by the people we meet and rebuked by our own consciences.

But even more important, the Holy Spirit Himself is deeply grieved, weeps holy tears over our religious fakery and instructs us in a better way—by the path of renewal through sincere repentance. He says:

God resists the proud, but gives grace to the humble. Therefore submit to God. Resist the devil and he will flee from
you. Draw near to God and He will draw near to you.
Cleanse your hands, you sinners; and purify your hearts,
you double-minded. Lament and mourn and weep! Let your
laughter be turned to mourning and your joy to gloom.
Humble yourselves in the sight of the Lord, and He will lift
you up. (James 4:6–10)

Thus, you do not need to continue as one of those whom
T. S. Eliot has called the "hollow men." Ask the Holy Spirit
to make you willing to be searched by God (Ps. 139:23–24).
Do not expect the process of searching to be always painless
and pleasant. No, hardly. But you will begin to have the joy
of a clear conscience and a deepening fellowship with Christ.
As you learn to thirst after Christ and drink of Him, you
will find the living waters of the Holy Spirit flowing through
you (John 7:37–39). No longer will you be merely existing,
you will be living—and from you waters will overflow into
other lives.

2

Repentance and Its Counterfeit

NEVERTHELESS, it is of the greatest importance that we understand what repentance really is and not confuse it with human effort to save ourselves by our own suffering. This is penance, not repentance. By the Spirit's help, the following discussion will make clear a number of major differences between penance and what the Bible calls "repentance to life" (Acts 11:18).

First, *penance centers on what people do.*

Penance is not merely a sacrament of the Roman Catholic Church. Rather, it is a religious attitude deeply rooted in the human heart which prompts people to attempt to pay for their own sins by good works and sufferings. Self-justification is the goal of this effort. In practice this means that humanity always has one more scheme for getting things right with God and their conscience. Sinners doing penance always say in their hearts, "Give me one more day, a new religious duty, another program, another set of human relationships or a better education, and then things will come right-side up."

They are preparationists—that is, sinners who are forever *getting ready* for grace. They want to make themselves worthy of grace so that God will reach out to them when once this work of preparation is completed. They say they are searchers who will not "cheapen grace" by taking any easy way out. They may expect to be saved through Christian education, by association with godly men and women or by acquiring clear conceptions of biblical doctrine.

But they do not know that this is a terrible insult to God and His grace. In their pride they are attempting the impossible. There is no way salvation can be absorbed from a Christian environment. There is no such thing as "growth into grace," because grace would then come as a result of human effort, and the free-gift character of grace would be destroyed.

Discipline, study and moral training cannot do the job, because human beings have a rotten root. So long as we look within ourselves for the source of our life, we know nothing of Christ. But if we are grafted into Christ, if we are rooted in Christ, then we can grow in grace. But we will never have the power to grow *into* grace as a work of moral reformation.

Therefore, anyone doing penance is sadly mistaken. Things cannot come right for such people. They cannot pay for their sins, because they poison all the best gifts of God. Send them to church and Christian schools for a lifetime and they will never come to know rightly a single thing about the living God and His mercy in Christ. For in their heart of hearts, they are proud—infinitely proud—perhaps without having the slightest idea that this is their basic problem. Having but themselves as the ground of their hope, they will not see the glory of Christ until the Spirit grants them "repentance to life," which includes a genuine turning from penance. In brief, they must repent of their penances.

This matter is very tricky. Self-deception goes right along with self-trust and self-justification (Jer. 17:9). You may say, "But you do not know how earnestly I pray for God's help. I have shed many tears over my sins." But friend, this cannot work, because at bottom you are still asking God to baptize your sin—to Christianize an essentially lustful heart by making you a little less nervous and a little more patient. The heavenly Father, however, does not hear your prayers, because you are in reality asking Him for help so that you can continue to live a life which is independent of God.

What these people seek from God is enough grace to be strong in themselves. They do not need or want a constant flow of water from heaven.

Therefore, they must intensify their own efforts even as they ask for divine aid. They think things go badly because they have not done enough. They must therefore do more of the same, but do it better and more often. Now they begin to engage in penance with a vengeance. If their instincts are strongly religious, they give themselves to what the New Testament calls "will worship"—worship which originates with the human will and not with the will of the Father (Col. 2:20–23). They go to religious services more frequently and may even physically beat themselves as well as lacerate their soul with thorns and briars of reproach. They may become a Sunday school teacher, a trustee of the church or a minister—all with the purpose of atoning for a guilty conscience.

If they have mystical tendencies, they may be drawn to

some form of Eastern religion in which "self-abasement and severity to the body" have become a fine art. If they follow the way of Zen, for example, they will seek to deny not only the demands of the body, but also the very mental processes which make them people in the image of God.

But the repentant person repudiates this whole process with its self-justification and pretense. For truly repentant sinners have discovered, through the renewing work of the Holy Spirit, that all their doing is full of sin. Their doing is the source of their wretched emptiness, their black depression and their self-despising. But now they have come undone. They turn from their sinful doing and trust in what Christ has done. This is the essence of repentance. Listen to Isaiah. He knows what it is to repent. Pierced to the heart by the knowledge of his sins, he cries out, "Woe is me, for I am undone!" (Isa. 6:5).

Second, *penance focuses on what people see and feel within themselves.*

Penance is centered in human emotions and perceptions. But repentance to life is God-centered.

The radical difference between the two can be made very clear by comparing Mark Twain's life as set forth in his *Autobiography* with the experience of Isaiah previously mentioned. Twain, in his *Autobiography*, has recalled the "repentances" of his youth which were powerfully stimulated by every public tragedy that occurred in Hannibal. He wrote:

> Those were awful nights, nights of despair, nights charged with the bitterness of death. After each tragedy I recognized the warning and repented; repented and begged; begged like a coward, begged like a dog.[1]

These repentings—actually worldly regrets—put the

young Twain under a heavy burden. His nights were filled with terror, especially after the killing of a man named Smarr one noonday in the streets of Hannibal. "Some thoughtful idiot," he recalls, "placed a great family Bible spread open on the profane old man's breast." For a long time afterwards, Twain was plagued by the memory of that awful scene, and as a consequence, often in his dreams he "gasped and struggled for breath under the crush of the vast book"[2] as though he were in Smarr's place.

Give it a glance only and it might seem that Mark Twain was experiencing genuine repentance toward God. He was certainly sensitive to his own moral rottenness. But his self-reflections were essentially just that—self-reflections. He was only sorry for himself, not sorry for sin against a holy and loving God. Accordingly, we must see that his confession of depravity was motivated principally by self-pity which became the basis for the bitter atheism of later books like *The Mysterious Stranger.*

Actually, his confession of sin was a thinly disguised criticism of God. What right does God have to place the weight of a vast book like the Bible on the chests of sinners? After all, God made human nature the way it is. If people do all human nature can do, what more is to be expected? In effect they ask, "If I have done all I can, why has not God done all He could?"

As a natural consequence, those doing penance will see God as owing them a debt; living in self-pity, they become almost unshakably convinced that if there is any forgiving to do, they must forgive God for making them such rotten sinners. People who do this are throwing away their eternal souls. They are willfully locking God out of their lives.

What a joy to turn from this corrosive prometheanism and meet a repentant sinner like Isaiah! Already we have learned from Isaiah 6 that the essence of repentance is to come "undone." But now the why of this must be made sharp and clear. Isaiah saw God. Let me repeat that: Isaiah saw God. Here is the perfect cure for sinners who say they despise their sinfulness, but who—if the truth were known—love every bit of it and even find perverse pleasure in the guilty misery it brings.

So hear Isaiah's brief but powerful confession: "Woe is me, for I am undone! Because I am a man of unclean lips, and I dwell in the midst of a people of unclean lips. For my eyes have seen the King, the LORD of hosts" (Isa. 6:5).

Isaiah is not half-guilty or half-lost. Because his eyes have looked upon the King, he is completely "undone," that is, "lost" or even "dead." Thus, the knowledge of God has brought a new knowledge of self. It is a breaking in from the outside by the entirely unexpected. Having beheld the Lord lifted up in majestic splendor, Isaiah is overwhelmed by awareness of the guilt of his lips. The burning ones (seraphim) shake the temple with the power of their praise: "Holy, holy, holy is the LORD of hosts; the whole earth is full of His glory!" (Isa. 6:3). Before this, Isaiah's lips had only mechanically praised God. His thanksgiving had been only talk. His words had gone up to heaven, but his heart and thoughts had remained below.

Heaven sings the holiness of the mighty King, and all the earth shows forth the glory of His wisdom, power, eternity, justice and lovingkindness. But Isaiah has sinned against "the glory" by his failure to praise the Lord for His great being and marvelous works.

Thus, Isaiah has sinned and come short of the glory of God (Rom. 3:23). Perhaps he also slandered people and gossiped with his lips, but the most terrible thing about him is that hardness of heart, that unbelief, which is unthankful and gives the glory of God to the creature (Rom. 1:21–23).

Humanity has an immense pride. This is the basis of the self-pity which leads people to condemn God for what seems to them bad management of human affairs. But one real meeting with the living God puts all this self-righteous junk into its true perspective. You just don't argue with holy fire. You submit to it.

Third, *penance always leaves the sinner powerless and imprisoned.*

The contrition of an Isaiah differs from worldly regret in that it goes deep into the heart, into the very springs of a person's life (Zech. 12:10–14). Repentant people see that even their prayers were the manifestation of a deep inner lie. But such repentance does not leave them guilt-ridden and powerless. For the sure mark of authentic repentance is boldness and joyous enthusiasm for the things of God. So Isaiah, touched by the cleansing fires of grace, stands confidently in the presence of the living God and joyfully accepts a most difficult missionary task. "Here am I!" he cries. "Send me" (Isa. 6:8).

Similarly, when Peter is called to be an apostle at the time of the great draught of fish, he is brought to a fruitful repentance. "Depart from me, for I am a sinful man, O Lord!" is his cry (Luke 5:8). But he need not fear. Real humbling awareness of our sinful weakness is an excellent place for missionaries to begin. To such the Lord draws very near and takes them gently by the hand, saying, "Do not be afraid. From now on you will catch men" (Luke 5:10).

But why is penance so frustrating? Simple. Penance does not work because it is founded upon self-trust. But repentance unto life is fused with trust in Christ as the all-sufficient mediator between God and humanity. And Christ always succeeds where human self-effort fails.

As one pastor expressed it, you would not ask for one side of a dollar bill, and no more would you seek repentance apart from faith or faith apart from repentance. Consequently, the preaching of repentance toward God must never be separated from preaching faith in Christ.

But there is a trap here which witnessing Christians must avoid. Christians with a respect for the Puritan tradition are especially prone to fall into it because they feel more strongly than others the necessity of preaching repentance and the law of God. This is most right and proper. However, the devil is exceedingly cunning and can easily introduce confusion at this point.

What happens is that the preacher and those who hear may confuse conviction of sin with coming to Christ. Now conviction of sin must *accompany* salvation, but conviction of sin is not salvation. We preach the Law to bring people to the knowledge of God's wrath against sin, but their response to the Law does not save them.

Let me explain. In the great invitational passages of Scripture, the exhortation is not to thirst, i.e., to acquire a conviction of sin. Instead, the command is for sinners to *drink* of Christ (John 7:37, Isa. 55:1–2). Scripture does not say that the way of salvation is to make yourself heavy with your sins. Instead, the invitation from the Lord is, "Come to Me, all you who labor and are heavy laden" (Matt. 11:28).

Conviction of sin by itself is not repentance. Conviction

of sin apart from turning to Christ has no value whatsoever. The Law and its effects are never saving. To come to Christ, to drink of Christ, is to believe in Him and be saved by Him alone. Salvation comes from union with the Lord through faith and nothing else.

This does not mean the Law has no value in bringing people to Christ. For example, Jesus exposes the particular sins of the Samaritan woman. She has broken the seventh commandment (John 4:16–18, Exod. 20:14). But Jesus does not urge her to enter a state of salvation through meditation upon her sins. Rather, He points her to Himself as the Water of Life. After all, the best way to make dry sinners feel thirst is to show them the cool, clean, fresh water which came down from heaven.

This means everything to the life of the church and to the one who is groping in the dark for Christ.

If conviction of sin is demanded as though this were the goal of things, if human unrighteousness is exposed apart from faith in Christ, then people will be left suspended in a state of penance and will return to pre-Reformation misery, with salvation made entirely unstable because it is founded on what human beings do to recover themselves.

Sinners in such a state have no way of knowing whether God loves them and will receive them to His heart. Psychologically and morally, all is left dark and shoreless. When sin is exposed apart from the promises of God, reality for the one outside of the Lord becomes increasingly inverted and twisted. The aching conscience cannot possibly find relief in this way.

But, praise God, there is no such thing as salvation by grimness! Instead, salvation is, to use John Newton's words, "costly and free." It cost God everything, yet it comes free and unearned to the sinner. It brings health and peace to the soul.

A believing repentance means that the sinner has passed from darkness into the light of God's kingdom. The irrationality of life without God is supplanted by a new sanity. The person has "come to himself" (see Luke 15:17). No longer are such persons guilt-ridden slaves on the edge of the abyss. The sorrow of their heart arises from conviction of sin which, being mixed with faith, brings them back to God. In this return prodigals abandon the delusion that they can act as though they are the creator of all. Now they see that they have no resources in themselves. What before seemed the essence of reasonableness is now recognized as the height of madness. In their state of rebellious insanity, they had experienced, in Geerhardus Vos' words, "a detachment of the spiritual consciousness from its center in God."[3]

Now they have tears of joy. Having returned to God as the center of life, they discover through faith that the Father's house has all the resources to meet our deepest needs—resources of forgiveness, cleansing of heart, eternal life, wisdom, love, joy and peace.

It is too much!

Fourth and last, *penance seeks out a human priest other than Christ.*

Since legalists are at best only pretending to go to God through Christ, they are in a desperate position. They feel deeply sorry for themselves, and in their self-pity they seek out comforters to incorporate into their system of self-trust. Such comforters, frequently respected religious leaders, are expected to do the work of Christ, God's only mediator.

All too often religious leaders are flattered into accepting the role of priest by sympathetic parishioners who admire their gifts and graces. In accepting this role, they harm themselves and the ones for whom they attempt to mediate. It must be recognized that they are sinners and may love people's honor and praise more than they know.

But the problem is even broader and deeper than pastors and their relationships with the members of their congregations. Christians who witness with power and effectiveness will find that others will look to them to do the work of Christ for them. For instance, as the pastor must take care not to become priest to needy people in the congregation, so the youth worker must take care not to become priest to the young people. The evangelist must follow suit with new converts.

Because most of this is unconscious, it is all the more dangerous. We are not to make men and women our own disciples, but to make them disciples of the Lord. Therefore, repentance means that people must turn from trusting in empty cisterns like ourselves and thirst and drink from Christ alone (John 7:37–38).

Pastors and Christian workers are not merely to accept this as an interesting insight which is mildly relevant to their work. It is, in fact, a matter of spiritual life and death. People today use priests, pastors, rabbis, psychiatrists, teachers, parents and devout friends as substitutes for Christ. Sometimes when the individualized priests fail, they will convert abstractions, like "youth," into their priest. Future-oriented, they place their hope with the children, thinking that they will build a better tomorrow.

It is important to recognize that the search for priests has been greatly intensified in modern society by the breakdown of the family and the churches. Modern education and psychology have also played a very important role. They have put the human ego under the microscope, thus making modern people intensely aware of themselves. Often students are so sensitized by self-awareness that they almost seem to me like people born without skin. They are all nerve ends. They are urgently looking for relief from the burdens of self as well as for a purpose in life.

If you are in a position of spiritual leadership, *do not direct these seekers to yourself.* Send them instead to Christ. Bathe them in your prayers and your love. Open your home and your heart to them. But make yourself understood, and in loving humility be very bold about it: They are not going to find their salvation in you.

Does the young man lack spiritual power because he is doing penance for sexual sins? Is that undisciplined girl on drugs functioning like a watch with a broken spring that no amount of winding helps? Is the person a "Christian," confident of knowing the Lord, but without fruit warranting the assurance?

Well, tell them the facts. You are a sinner like they are. The only place you get grace is from Christ. To make this point very strong, more than once in our home we have taken young people by the hand and placed them alone in a room with a Bible and the admonition, "Don't use me as your priest. Go to Christ alone."

Encourage them by your own example. Let them see how you wrestle with your sins and how you break down your own proud defensiveness through honest, heart-searching prayer. Let them see you experience the joys of forgiveness received from God as a free gift based upon the sacrifice of His Son.

A passage of Scripture which can be of great help here is Psalm 32. This is a joy psalm. It begins with "Blessed is he whose transgression is forgiven" (Ps. 32:1) and ends with "Be glad in the LORD and rejoice, you righteous; and shout for joy, all you upright in heart!" (Ps. 32:11).

What's all the shouting about? Just this: God has done something for David that is altogether astonishing in its beauty. Through atonement by sacrifice, God has freely forgiven David his sins. The forgiveness is total. Not a single sin remains after God blots out his evil record. Through Christ righteousness is reckoned to David without works (Rom. 4:6–8). This is justification by faith alone.

But there is something more. Before this David had been acting "like the horse or like the mule, which have no understanding" (Ps. 32:9). That is, he had been behaving as a non-sinner. He was defensive, beastly. He had nothing to confess. But he was also utterly miserable without fully realizing it. "When I kept silent, my bones grew old through my groaning all the day long" (Ps. 32:3).

But his joy came back when he went to God and confessed his sin and received full pardon through grace: "I acknowledged my sin to You, and my iniquity I have not hidden. I said, 'I will confess my transgressions to the LORD,' and You forgave the iniquity of my sin" (Ps. 32:5).

The lesson in all this is that we do not need to live with a festering conscience. There is a Mediator appointed of God, even the Lord Jesus. Take your sins to God through Jesus. This High Priest intercedes for repentant sinners on the basis of His own perfect record. All He requires is a believing honesty, a willingness to trust our sins to Him without self-deceit or self-righteousness.

3

What Is
True Repentance?

SO FAR we have seen from Scripture that sinners must repent so that they may be near to God and no longer in a state of death. We have stressed that God has not called us to be attorneys acting in our own defense, but beggars humbled before the throne of grace, refusing to leave until bread is forthcoming.

But the most powerful reason for turning from our sin to serve God has yet to be given. At first, it may not seem to have any weight at all. The Bible, however, makes much of it. This motivation for changing one's mind and life-direction is *the lordship of the crucified Savior.*

All the great passages in Luke and Acts which deal with the imperative to repent are rooted in this exaltation of the Lord. In the Lukan account of the Great Commission, it is the resurrected Christ who says "that repentance and remission of sins should be preached in His name to all nations, beginning at Jerusalem" (Luke 24:47). Paul warns the Athenians that they must repent because the resurrected Christ will judge the world (Acts 17:30–31). In explaining his ministry to King Agrippa, Paul says he "declared first to those in Damascus and in Jerusalem, and throughout all the region of Judea, and then to the Gentiles, that they should repent, turn to God, and do works befitting repentance" (Acts 26:20). This ministry of repentance was given to Paul by the resurrected Lord on the Damascus road (Acts 26:12–18).

Luke also explains what it was at Pentecost that brought conviction of sin to the hardened Jews. Peter charged them with crucifying Jesus "by the hand of lawless men" (Acts 2:23, ASV). But the magnitude of this sin becomes apparent only when Israel discovers what God has done with the Man whom they have killed. "Therefore," he says, "let all the house of Israel know assuredly that God has made this Jesus, whom you crucified, both Lord and Christ" (Acts 2:36).

Peter's audience is appalled by this announcement, supported as it is by the flaming demonstration of power given by the Spirit of God. In the face of God's deed in raising Christ from the dead and making Him Lord of all, their sin takes on its true, hideous color. They have killed the "Prince of life" (Acts 3:15)! No wonder that "when they heard this, they were cut to the heart, and said to Peter and the rest of the apostles, 'Men and brethren, what shall we do?'" (Acts 2:37)!

This sovereign Lord does not, however, confine His call to unbelievers. Christian sins are not venial. Sin is sin wherever it is found, and it is worse to find it in the Christian. Therefore, He especially zeroes in on loveless, complacent and compromising members of the household of faith. For example, He says bluntly to the loveless, but carefully ortho-dox, Ephesians, "Remember therefore from where you have fallen; *repent* and *do* the first works" (Rev. 2:5).

The vision is not of the effeminate, long-haired Jesus of popular religious art. But He who commands repentance is none other than the One who is the First and the Last, Alpha and Omega. In the book of Revelation, He is both the Son of Man and the Ancient of Days in one exalted Person. Behold His majesty:

> I saw seven golden lampstands, and in the midst of the seven lampstands One like the Son of Man, clothed with a garment down to the feet and girded about the chest with a golden band. His head and hair were white like wool, as white as snow, and His eyes like a flame of fire; His feet were like fine brass, as if refined in a furnace, and His voice as the sound of many waters. (Rev. 1:12–15)

In the presence of such a Lord, who can defend himself? John falls "at His feet as dead" and must be reassured by the loving touch of Jesus' right hand (Rev. 1:17). Here we learn that Jesus comes to us as the all-seeing Lord who searches every nook and cranny of the heart.

In the presence of this exalted Lord, self-defense is foolishness, but self-examination aided by the Holy Spirit is everything. Stated practically, our self-examination before the Lord must deal with two kinds of sins. For the purpose of easier understanding, we shall call one kind *branch-sins* and the other *root-sins*.

Branch-sins are those faults which others most quickly see in us. They are the sins which most obviously get in the way of relationships with others. They are branch-sins, however, not because they are little sins—but because branches are more observable than roots, and because branches derive their life and strength from hidden roots.

Take laziness as an example. Rarely do you hear anyone say much about it. But laziness is one of the most wide-spread and flagrant sins in modern life. Since World War II, a generation of people has swarmed onto the stage of history whose members do not like to work and, in some cases, are proud of it. At present we are experiencing something like an epidemic of moral vagrancy, with more and more people moving restlessly from job to job, and increasing numbers of young people hating the very idea of sustained work. There are professing Christians among their number as well, who claim that their drifting is in obedience to the Holy Spirit, when in fact they have confused the leading of the Spirit with romantic impulse.

The biblical teaching on work must be made clear. Labor is one of God's creation ordinances. At the beginning the Creator made work an integral part of human life and service (Gen. 1:28–30, 2:15). Since the fall into sin, work has come under God's curse, and people no longer understand its full significance (Gen. 3:17–19). However as a consequence of Christ's resurrection victory, He was constituted the Lord of a new creation. Now this risen Lord requires that Christians live out their lives as new creations. This means that they stop stealing and freeloading and go to work so that they may have the means to give to others (Eph. 4:17–28, especially v. 28).

It is because of sin that the biblical concept of *vocation* (work as a calling from God) has been replaced by the modern concept of life as a happy *vacation* from work responsibility. And the source of the resistance to work can go deep into the hidden motives of the heart.

Behind the on-again, off-again work habits of our day is a worldly pride. Fused with this pride is the fear of work that exhausts lazy people before they even lift a finger. Furthermore, interpenetrating the whole complex of human sin is the negative power of unbelief, which constantly feeds our rebellious opposition to God.

We saw this in the case of a young woman who was brought into our home in a very weakened physical and emotional state. We were told that her emotional problems were so serious that there was danger she might die.

What were we to do? It was clear that she had only consented to stay with us because she was ill. Nevertheless, she was convinced that her life would soon come right-side up. After all, she was a devout fundamentalist who had already "accepted" Christ.

After she gained some strength, we laid out a program of light work and household responsibilities for her. But they didn't get done. She resented each task when it became monotonous. Work literally made her sick. Desperate, we had no place to go but to God. From Him we learned to deal truly with her in love. In effect we said, "You must get up and work even when you do not feel like it, because this is what Christ commands." However, it was like pushing a string. She had no confidence that she could do anything well. Outwardly she would accept a responsibility, but underneath she rebelled against any task that crossed her will.

As we daily repented of similar sins in our own lives, the love of Christ entered into us with special power. We began to understand and freely to forgive. There was nothing in her that was not in us also. The difference, however, was that she knew nothing of the joy and power which comes through a believing repentance.

Finally, in a dramatic confrontation she was converted. She met Christ the Lord and saw what His claims really were. The resistance to discipline was broken and a new life emerged. But for this to happen, the Lord had to dig up the root sins of rebellious pride and unbelief. It is her contention that before this uprooting took place, she was trusting in "eternal security" and not in Christ for salvation.

Now she is able to work a full-time job and no longer needs the shelter of our home. When strength permits, she willingly volunteers to come over and help out with household chores. In a new way she lives by faith, and the awareness of the love of God so fills her life that now my wife and I really find ourselves being taught by this vital Christian. This is not to suggest the young woman is turned into a super-Christian. But the difference is fundamental, so much so that it is difficult even to identify the new person with the old.

This transformation also illustrates the necessity of preaching repentance as a total surrender to a sovereign Lord. Evil is a totality. But Christ is a total Savior, able to redeem us from evil as a world system under the dominion of Satan.

Thanks be to God that He has made Jesus both Lord and Christ! Otherwise the dominion of sin would keep us permanently enslaved until its wages issued in death (Rom. 6:23). But the Lord gives what He commands. Repentance, certainly, is our responsibility. God does not repent any more than He believes. However, repentance is also a gift sovereignly granted by God (see Acts 11:16–18, Jer. 17:14, Lam. 5:21). It is but the humanward side of that divine renewing which comes as a free gift from heaven.

B. B. Warfield sums it up neatly:

Man repents, makes amendment, and turns to God. But it is by God that men are renewed, brought forth, born again into newness of life. The transformation which to human vision manifests itself as a change of life . . . resting upon a radical change of mind . . . , to Him who searches the heart and understands all the movements of the human soul is known to be a creation . . . of God, beginning in a new birth from the Spirit . . . and issuing in a new divine product . . . , created in Christ Jesus, into good works prepared by God beforehand that they may be walked in (Eph. 2:10).[4]

Be encouraged then, fellow believer. In calling you to daily repentance, the Lord Jesus is not simply giving you good advice. He is saying, "If you are a child of mine, you must continue to repent." He does not say to reform your human nature inherited from Adam. Instead, He says to "put to death your members which are on the earth" (Col. 3:5). And dying is not easy. Nor, as we will see from Scripture, does it all happen at one's conversion.

Now there is grand encouragement here. The putting to death of the flesh—ongoing repentance—is not something reserved for the select few. For repentance, in the larger use of the New Testament word, includes trust in Christ which unites the believer to the Lord in His death, burial and resurrection (Rom. 6:1–11; Col. 2:9–12, 3:1–4). So to be in Christ is to be in possession of the power to put to death the lusts of the flesh (Col. 3:5), to put off vicious habits like uncontrolled anger, slander and lying (Col. 3:8–9), and to put on the qualities of love, kindness, meekness and patience which identify a person as one of the elect of God (Col. 3:12–17).

Christians have veered off the biblical path here in a number of ways. Some talk about the sinfulness of humanity without dealing with particular sins. Others limit themselves to a generalized confession of sins during worship that amounts to little more than a solemn liturgical formula. I have rarely seen anyone undergo fundamental change through it. It seldom puts to death anything other than our consciences.

But what concerns me most are those Christians who have gone so far as to deny that repentance should include the pain that accompanies particular confessions of sin to God. Lewis Sperry Chafer, for example, believes that the word *metanoia* (repentance) contains nothing of sorrow for sin. He states that "the word means *a change of mind*. The common practice of reading into this word the thought of sorrow and heart anguish for sin is responsible for much confusion in the field of Soteriology."[5]

To be sure, Chafer is right when he says that *metanoia* has for its primary meaning a change of mind, and his concern to steer away from mixing penance with repentance is deserving of praise. But a Spirit-wrought sorrow of heart for sin is not penance. If this were so, God would not tell us how He delights in the tears of repentant sinners (Ps. 34:18, 51:17).

For it all depends upon what kind of grief is in the heart. There are worldly tears, and there are tears from the convicting power of Christ's Spirit. "Worldly grief" produces death, but "godly sorrow produces repentance leading to salvation, not to be regretted" (2 Cor. 7:10). James bluntly tells his readers to "lament and mourn and weep" (James 4:9). Joel, the prophet whose vision was centered on the coming of the Spirit, connects turning to God "with fasting, with weeping, and with mourning" (Joel 2:12). And Zechariah is the boldest of all. He sees the outpouring of the Spirit as leading sinners to a vision of the crucified Christ, with the result that the age of the Spirit will be characterized by a mourning for sin unlike that of any previous epoch (Zech. 12:10–14).

John Colquhoun summed up the difference in the quaint but vivid language of another century:

> It, Godly sorrow of Biblical repentance, is also a lively grief, a grief that quickens the soul. The sorrow of the world works death; it indisposes a man for activity in duty. But godly sorrow quickens a man to the spiritual performance of duty. The former arises from slavish dread, which chills and stiffens the soul, so renders it unfit for action, the latter from faith and love, which warm the heart, and dispose it to be ardent and active.[6]

It is simply impossible for someone to meet the Lord of glory in the full revelation of His majesty and not be grieved by particular sins and want to confess them. This was the experience of Job, David, Isaiah, Peter and the hearers of Peter at Pentecost. But at the same time, the honest unburdening of the heart to God brings joy into the life which was never known before. Thus, Simon the Pharisee is a "small" sinner who has little or nothing to confess. But the prostitute who wept at Jesus' feet was deeply grieved by her multitude of sins. To this penitent believer Jesus said, "Your faith has saved you. Go in peace" (Luke 7:50).

Therefore, take care not to rob someone of "godly grief" over sin. For if you rob them of the grief, you will also rob them of the joy which comes as a consequence of a hearty repentance.

4

Repentance and the Spirit-filled Life

IN THESE days much of the church resembles a desert (Jer. 17:5–6). But in the midst of the desert there is a moving of the dry bones. People are beginning to see that their souls are very dry. Therefore, they are seeking after an answer. In many instances the Spirit of God appears to be moving them to seek the abundant life which Jesus promised His sheep (John 10:10).

Nonetheless, there is great danger that the concern for new life will center largely on an emotional experience rather than on the risen Lord. Historically, the various pneumatic movements have put forward the view that emotional intensity practically equals the presence of the Holy Spirit. But this can turn into a disastrous mistake. For example, the Welsh revival of 1904 had a good deal of its long-term influence dissipated because of the emphasis on experience rather than on the preaching of the Christ of Scripture.

The heart of the problem appears to be that Christians often think of the filling of the Spirit largely in quantitative terms, as though the believer were a quart jar one-third full. In this view the coming of the Spirit consists in the filling of the jar to the brim, usually through an experience of great emotional power.

In all this longing there is commonly a hunger for a life which is delivered at one stroke from all sin and temptation. This longing is not to be despised. But it will not be fully realized until the believer is fully glorified at the time of his death or at the return of the Lord. Furthermore, the serious danger is that those who seek the Spirit in this way will shift their reliance from the daily working of the Spirit to a previous landmark experience of great emotional intensity.

What happens is that people with this experience in their background can become secretly proud that they are "spiritual" Christians of a special class. They no longer look to Christ in love (2 Cor. 3:18). Instead, they mount a pedestal and quench the Holy Spirit, denying the reality of the sin which yet remains in them and which must be put to death by active reliance on Christ (Rev. 3:14–22, Col. 3:15).

At present there are some teachings that push their adherents in this direction. They emphasize intense religious experience, and they tend to stress sin as human *actions* without taking sufficiently into account sin as a *state* of the heart. These ingredients of perfectionism are dangerous.

The hazard here should be obvious. People who believe this know they have the Holy Spirit. And they are right. But they no longer can freely admit that they must confess their pride and unbelief on a daily basis. They also may begin to think themselves qualified to serve as priests for others.

Moreover, those they "help" will often admire them—for a time. For just as they are soft on their own sins, so they will be soft on the sins of others. Or if they *are* severe with people's sins, they will only deal with surface matters, for those who do not have the courage to look into the depths of their own hearts cannot see clearly into the heart of another.

Quickly their lives will lose their power, and they will be plunged into all the evasions of penance. Increasingly, people will turn away from them and listen less and less to their witness, which is drifting ever deeper into sham.

What we must see is that God never promised to transform us into super-Christians who would never again sin and never again need to repent. He never promised anybody strength apart from continued dependence upon Himself (Jer. 10:23, John 15:5).

For example, God mightily inspired energy in Paul (Col. 1:29), but this power did not come from himself. For the apostle was deeply impressed by his own weakness as a man. In himself he was completely impotent. But God's grace is made perfect in weakness so that all the glory might be God's and not ours (2 Cor. 12:9–10, 13:3–4).

Therefore, I want to set down two closely related criteria for the Spirit-filled life: The first is sincere love to the Lord Jesus Christ as the gift of the Father's love, and the second is a genuine repentance which causes us to be broken down before God.

First, according to Scripture, the presence of love in the Christian life is a sure evidence of the fullness of the Holy Spirit. To understand this as a promise to you personally, turn to your Bible and read John 14:15–24 (a related passage is John 16:27).

From verse 16 we learn that the Holy Spirit will be given to the disciples because Christ will pray to the Father. Hence, Jesus promises them, "I will not leave you orphans" (John 14:18).

But there is something that the disciples must do and be if they are to receive the full presence of the Father. This concerns their response to Jesus. The Lord says, "He who has My commandments *and keeps them*, it is he who loves Me. And he who loves Me will be loved by My Father, and I will love him and manifest Myself to him" (John 14:21).

Catch the loving fire of Jesus' words. Loving obedience to Jesus by His disciples attracts the love of both the Father and the Son. Jesus specifically promises that whoever loves Him will be loved in turn by the Lord and will receive His presence in a special way. Jesus says, "I will love him and *manifest Myself* to him."

In verse 23 this manifestation is further explained. "If anyone loves me," Jesus adds, "he will keep My word; and My Father will love him, and We will come to him and make Our home with him." Loving obedience results in the Father and the Son coming into the believer's life in a fuller way. The language is strong. The Father and the Son will move in whenever a believer looks in love to Jesus. The Father cannot resist fellowship with His own dear children when they embrace Christ in all His offices as prophet, priest and king.

As a believer saved by grace through faith, you know that all love to you began first with God. In eternity the Father elected you in Christ without any consideration whatsoever of your merits or response to God's working (Eph. 1:3–4). His love initiated the whole program of salvation while you were yet a sinner (Rom. 5:8, 1 John 4:19). But if you wish the continued fellowship of this love, adore Jesus Christ and love Him with all your heart. Show your love by obeying Him and you will find your life abounding in spiritual power.

Do you wish to "be filled with all the fullness of God" (Eph. 3:19)? Through faith you must study how to love Christ more. In Paul's thought, love to Jesus and the "fullness of God" go together. Listen:

> For this reason I bow my knees to the Father of our Lord Jesus Christ, from whom the whole family in heaven and earth is named, that He would grant you, according to the riches of His glory, to be strengthened with might through His Spirit in the inner man, that Christ *may dwell in your hearts* through faith; that you, being *rooted and grounded in love*, may be able to comprehend with all the saints what is the width and length and depth and height—*to know the love of Christ* which passes knowledge; that you may be *filled with all the fullness of God.* (Eph. 3:14–19)

We must therefore see that the Spirit of truth present at Pentecost is, first of all, a Spirit of love leading people into disciplined obedience to Christ. He is a missionary Spirit who draws us into the fellowship of the saints by causing redeemed sinners to love Christ and one another. As those in Christ grow in love to one another, this love becomes highly visible (John 13:34–35, 17:22–23). It magnetizes men and women to the church of God.

Here then is the true charismatic movement. It is centered on the excellent way of love (1 Cor. 12:31–13:13). Outward signs and wonders prove little as to the reality of the Holy Spirit's presence (Matt. 7:21–23). In particular, "speaking in tongues" is a phenomenon to be found in non-Christian religions, and therefore can hardly be a convincing proof of the Spirit's presence.

Consequently, forget every quantitative concept of the Holy Spirit's presence. For to have the Holy Spirit in you is to have more of Christ in you, to be more like Christ and to bear the fruit of the Spirit which comes through faith in Christ and His merits (Gal. 5:22–23).

The second (and intimately related) criterion of the Spirit's presence is repentance. Since a good deal has already been said in this study concerning repentance and the Holy Spirit, let me simply cite one passage of Scripture to demonstrate how the gift of the Spirit and man's act of repentance were identified in the minds of God's people after Pentecost.

In Acts 11 we have Peter's explanation of his conduct in eating with recently converted Gentiles, an action which shocked the sensibilities of the Jerusalem church. But Peter defends himself by explaining that God had given the gift of the Holy Spirit to the Gentiles "as He gave us when we believed on the Lord Jesus Christ" (Acts 11:17). In response to this disclosure, the believers "glorified God, saying, 'Then God has also granted to the Gentiles repentance to life'" (Acts 11:18).

Note the process of thought. The church at Jerusalem identifies the Gentile reception of the Spirit through faith in Christ with repentance. Here, as elsewhere in Acts, the word "repentance" (*metanoia*) is used in a very broad sense, virtually as a synonym for conversion. The emphasis falls on the radical character of the change from death to life, from the proud delusions of the pagans to a humble dependence upon the living God for salvation. Hence, this passage makes absolutely clear that the New Testament church saw the fullness of the Spirit to be the same as a state of repentance for sin.

But what is true of the first turning (conversion) of the sinner to the Lord must continue throughout the Christian life. There must be a daily conversion of the heart to God (Col. 2:6). And the more you deepen your repentance, the more room you have in your heart for the rivers of living water. The more you know that you are stained to the bone with selfish impulses, the more you see how you hold out against the will of the Lord, then the more you will go to Christ as a thirsty sinner who finds deeper cleansing, more life and greater joy through the Spirit.

We have said that love and repentance are positive proof of the fullness of the Spirit's presence. But what is the vital connection between the two?

The answer is found by looking into the heart of any child of God who is walking in loving obedience. It's exciting. Here you meet ardent love to Jesus because the believer has been "broken" down through repentance. Repentance prepares the way so that the Lord of glory can enter into the spirit and be adored as the new center of heavenly life. Before, such people were consumed by self-love, but once the Spirit convicted them of sin and turned them to the cross, self-love was crowded out by love to the Lord Jesus Christ.

5

Repentance
and the Carnal Christian

The issue should now be coming into sharp focus for you. The Bible challenges you to see that Christ brought in a new age, the age of the Spirit. In this new day of grace, repentant believers are powerfully transformed people. Weak in themselves, they are full of Christ. This is God's normal pattern.

This is what Peter had in view when he told his hearers at Pentecost, "Repent, and let every one of you be baptized in the name of Jesus Christ for the remission of sins; and you shall receive the gift of the Holy Spirit" (Acts 2:38). As used by Peter, repentance is our conversion to the name of Christ and includes faith. Having abandoned ourselves and all our own righteousness, we find perfect reconciliation to God by claiming Christ's death as payment for our sins. Apart from Christ's shed blood, repentance is an empty word, but with Christ it leads us into a state of pardon and our receiving the fullness of the Holy Spirit.

Fullness? At this point many Christians will see a conflict with the popular division of believers into two classes, carnal and spiritual. Obviously, the so-called carnal Christian is not full of the Holy Spirit and does not bow to the lordship of Christ. Is there something wrong with a teaching which uses these categories?

Let's now examine the rationale for this carnal/spiritual dichotomy. There are at least three reasons why this view of the Christian life is widely held by believers today.

First, the carnal/spiritual division is thought to be the plain teaching of 1 Corinthians 3:1–4. In this passage Paul rebukes the Corinthians for acting carnal rather than spiritual. Since he labels them as carnal, some have taken this to mean that there exists a permanent class of carnal Christians.

Second, the category of carnal Christian is said to be necessary in order to preserve the grace-character of the gospel against legalism. The fear is that an invitation to receive Christ as Lord as well as Savior implies that unconverted sinners must make themselves spiritual by their own effort, thus undermining free justification through faith in Christ alone.

Third, there are concerns of the heart which seem to lead many believers to support the classification of Christians into spiritual and carnal. For reasons of charity, they wish to identify "backslidden" friends and relatives as carnal Christians. Often these people have made a commitment to Christ at some point in the past, but since then have failed to live the Christian life.

However, having considered these reasons, I contend that a careful consideration of the carnal/spiritual dichotomy will reveal that it has little basis in Scripture.

Reflect on the context of 1 Corinthians 3:1–4. In popular theology, to be a carnal Christian is to be a rather worldly believer who is not filled with the Spirit. Such people are not submitted to the lordship of Christ, and the Spirit is not powerfully active in their lives. But the Pauline argument in 1 Corinthians is *based* upon the indwelling of the Spirit in these believers! They are, he reasons, to be holy *because* they are inhabited by the Spirit of holiness, who is God's own transforming presence.

Move down the chapter to verse sixteen. Paul asks, "Do you not know that you are God's temple and that God's Spirit dwells in you?" Paul does not tell them, "You are on a carnal level of Christian development. What you need is to experience the baptism of the Spirit." No, he says, "You are already holy through the Spirit. Why then are you acting as though you didn't have the Spirit?"

The scandal is that they have become a contradiction in terms: They are spiritual people who are living as though they were not possessed of the Spirit. He states, "But you were washed, but you were sanctified, but you were justified in the name of the Lord Jesus and by the Spirit of our God" (1 Cor. 6:11). Therefore, stop backsliding!

That's the key term—backsliding. That's what Paul means when he calls them carnal. They are backsliders. Backsliding is not a category or a stage in Christian development, but it is living, unrepentant, in a state of sin on the part of those who know better. As such, it is an abomination to God and ought to be to us also.

Definitely, elements of carnality still plague the new Christian. The same can be said of the mature believer. But so long as God's people continue to repent and cling to Christ for growth in grace, they are not carnal in the Pauline sense. They are going forward—sometimes only creeping on hands and knees—but they are not sliding backward like stubborn brute beasts.

Then what about the problem of legalism? Will not emphasis on repentance and the lordship of Christ put us on the road to salvation by self-effort?

If this is a problem, it certainly did not trouble the apostles in the New Testament. In Acts 16:31, for example, Paul and Silas told the Philippian jailer, "Believe on the *Lord* Jesus Christ, and you will be saved, you and your household."

Why is the Philippian jailer commanded to believe in Christ as Lord and Savior? Because that is exactly what Christ is. He is inseparably *the Lord Jesus Christ.* By virtue of His resurrection victory He has become Lord of all (Matt. 28:18). So to be saved—what is it? Nothing could be plainer: "If you confess with your mouth *the Lord Jesus* and believe in your heart *that God has raised Him from the dead,* you will be saved" (Rom. 10:9).

Accordingly, salvation now begins to stand out as a much bigger and more wonderful thing than most contemporary believers see and understand. In this light we may conclude that in many instances people who think they are receiving a second work of grace are actually getting a first work of grace, namely, that passing from death to life that is conversion.

Let me illustrate. A young man reported that he had received a second work of grace which he called "the Spirit-filled life." He said that before this development he had assurance of faith, but that he did not enjoy worship, Bible reading or prayer. Nor did he have any feeling of love toward God. But afterward, he was filled with praise in worship. He now devours the Bible, witnesses fervently and begins to love God with his whole heart.

Although the young man at first resisted the idea, it is pretty clear that he was describing that conversion experience which the New Testament calls repentance to life. Obviously, the lordship of Christ stood at the heart of this Spirit-filled testimony. Praise God for that! But it is very likely that the young man was being evangelized by the Holy Spirit rather than receiving a new growth in grace.

It should, therefore, be fully understood that in the New Testament the lordship of Christ is the basis of evangelism. It underlies the Great Commission (Matt. 28:18–20), it stands at the center of Paul's great definition of the gospel (1 Cor. 15:3–5), and it is a truth heralded with flaming power at Pentecost (Acts 2:36). With respect to evangelism, G. Campbell Morgan says, "To preach the living lordship of Christ is to create the necessity for His cross."[7] His point is that most people won't take the cross seriously unless they know that Jesus actually rose again from the dead and now holds all power in His hands (Matt. 28:16–20).

Why then should anyone attack "lordship evangelism"?

One reason is that many believers still misconstrue repentance as a legalistic work of our own doing. Obviously, if repentance involves human self-effort, then it would destroy the stability of grace and throw a cloud over the glory of Christ's atonement. But, as has been stressed in this study, repentance has nothing to do with what we have done. Rather, it is our coming undone in respect to all human righteousness, followed by going outside ourselves in faith to Christ alone for salvation.

But there is a second reason why "lordship evangelism" has made some Bible-believing Christians nervous. The concern here does not seem to be entirely unwarranted. For if submitting to the lordship of Christ is understood as a process by which we attain holiness apart from union with Christ through faith, or as a kind of moral development by which we grow into grace, we may fall back into medieval moralism and justification by a mixture of grace and human works.

Therefore, take great care not to cloud matters in witnessing by implying that conversion must come as a climax to a long struggle through a dark tunnel. Specifically, it is unwise to teach that God ordinarily brings people to Himself over a long period of time. Such a conclusion could easily be misunderstood. It could imply that it is up to *us* to get ready for salvation.

Furthermore, such a judgment hardly receives support from the New Testament. In fact, a careful reading of the book of Acts and the Pauline epistles indicates that the opposite was often the case; that is, conversion followed right after the preaching of the gospel. Think of the immediate conversions at Pentecost. Conceivably, the church at Thessalonica came into being after a ministry of only three weeks by the apostle Paul (Acts 17:1–10). Also, practically all of the individual conversions mentioned by Luke in Acts— that of the Ethiopian eunuch, Sergius Paulus, Lydia, the Philippian jailer and the apostle Paul—appear to have been quickly and powerfully wrought by the Holy Spirit.

But having given this necessary warning about legalistic

misconstruction of Christ's lordship, we must insist that the fact of lordship remains.

Jesus is on the throne. He rules as a welcoming and enabling Lord. To repent and thus to come under His lordship is to be filled with the Holy Spirit. To believe in Him is to have so much of the Lord in you that you overflow. He who believes in Jesus has "a fountain of water springing up into everlasting life" (John 4:14).

Study John 7:37–39 carefully. In verse 37 thirsty sinners are challenged to come to Jesus and drink. This drinking is the equivalent of believing in Him, as verse 38 reveals. "He who believes in Me," says Jesus, "out of his heart will flow rivers of living water" (v. 38). After Pentecost this abundance will be normal for every believer, because the Spirit will be in the church (v. 39).

The practical implications are far-reaching. For one thing, there are many so-called "carnal Christians." They are not the easily discouraged "baby Christians" who need the assurances of grace. Instead, they are counting heavily on things like Christian heritage, church membership, mastery of an evangelical vocabulary, leadership position, orthodox belief or even a "born again" experience to get them into heaven. But they really do not understand Christ, nor do they yearn to know Him and His resurrection power. They do not seem to have repentance to life and saving faith. Their hearts are dominated by self rather than Christ. Some of them may be backsliders as were the Corinthians, but many more of them are simply people filled with religious talk.

More than once in His parables, Jesus warns about the possibility that a person may make a commitment to Christ that is superficial and not saving (Matt. 22:11–14, 25:1–13,

31–46, 7:21–27). The invitation goes out into the high-ways and byways, but not everyone who arrives at the great final banquet has the righteousness which accompanies repentance. To such, the Lord's words will come like dreadful thunder: "Friend, how did you come in here without a wedding garment?" (Matt. 22:12).

Can it be a favor to those who may be without a wedding garment to treat them as though they were lower-level Christians, when, by every test supplied in Scripture, these persons appear to be as cold and dead as a tombstone? My experience has been this: There is no greater stumbling block to the salvation of pseudo-Christians than the insistence of believing relatives and friends that the unsaved loved one is already in Christ.

It is biblical for me to examine myself to see whether or not I am in the faith (2 Cor. 13:5). Why then should it injure others to ask them in loving humility to join you in self-examination? If they find they are genuinely in Christ, they will rejoice to see what a firm foundation has been laid for them by the Father. If they should prove not to be in Christ, then their souls are alerted to their danger, and they have a wonderful opportunity to repent and trust in Jesus.

But I do not mean to imply for a moment that every believer's religious life should be modeled along the same lines. Christian piety can take many different forms. But whenever there is genuine life, this life will produce the fruit of the Spirit (Gal. 5:22). That is the whole point of Galatians. Faith and the Holy Spirit produce supernatural fruit, just as legalistic unbelief produces the works of the flesh.

Certainly, genuine believers like those at Corinth may for a time quench the Holy Spirit so that they come to resemble carnal Christians. But it is the nature of the authentic Christian to respond with repentance and deeds of righteousness when corrected by the Word. This is what happened to the Corinthians when they were shocked into wakefulness by the severe rebukes of the apostle Paul (2 Cor. 7:8–12). Thus, in calling down the Corinthians for their sinful conduct, Paul was demanding that they return posthaste to the Lord. He did not have the slightest intention of creating a permanent class of believers to be known as "carnal Christians" who do not bow before Christ as Lord. Nothing could have been further from the apostle's mind.

Thus it is that we may never accept carnal-mindedness as the fundamental feature for any individual believer's life or the characteristic of any class of Christians. For the carnal mind is at enmity with God and set in the way of death (see Rom. 8:6–8). Hence, if people are really carnally minded, they are lost and yet in their sins.

But what will be the effect of this biblical view of conversion on the number of converts?

At first glance, it might seem to reduce the number of conversions by frightening people off. After all, if you push repentance and the sovereign claims of Christ into the background, sinners might find it easier to receive Christ "only as Savior" because the demands seem lower.

Yet this thinking hardly measures up. Do you think that half a Christ is more attractive to a burdened conscience than a whole Christ? If the matter were explained to the thirsty soul, do you think the person would be content with a sip of water when the Lord offers Himself in all His overflowing fullness?

Honestly, I do not believe that any evangelical Christian

really wants quick and temporary responses to the gospel. But in contemporary evangelism we have unintentionally multiplied "converts" who slip through our hands like so much sand. Of course, there will always be some falling away. Many disciples turned away from our Lord (John 6:41–66), and the apostle Paul apparently saw defections even among fellow laborers in the gospel (2 Tim. 1:15, 2:17–18).

But this is not all that is going on at present. What is now being done that is so wrong is to assure people that they have eternal life, when *in many cases they don't.* In reality, this reduces the possibility of genuine conversions in two ways.

First, it deceives people who think they are converted and are not by giving them the Christian stamp. Although they are spiritually dead, they now tend to trust in doctrine and the "promises of God." How can they find Christ now? They are locked in. Sometimes their consciences trouble them about their spiritual impotence, but they cover over their doubts by taking a firmer grip on their concept of assurance.

Second, the presence of large numbers of unconverted "converts" in the church and society confuses the whole issue of what it means to be lost and saved. This actually prevents conversions by blurring the whole idea of the new life which Christ promises in abundance to His sheep (John 10:10). These so-called believers may have the best intention in the world, but they are very poor advertisements of the saving power of Christ.

For you cannot obey Christ without the power of Christ working in you. Without Him and His enabling grace, the obligations of Christian duty become oppressive legalism. This was Mark Twain's problem, and it is the problem of countless professing Christians today. So far as they are concerned, God, Christ, the Holy Spirit, the Word of God, faith, repentance and prayer can do nothing for them. No wonder such people are discouraged with Christ and the Christian faith.

Therefore, it is exceedingly important that we do not allow anything to blur the radical difference between the old and the new creation. To do so is to obscure the glory of the Christian hope and the transforming power of grace. We must give all the energy of faith to preaching that Christ of God who gives a totally new life with fullness of spiritual being. Modern men and women have burned themselves out with transitory experience—oriental religion, drugs, the occult and sexual perversion. We must not invite them to embrace Jesus as the latest fad. Instead, give them the full riches of the gospel of God, including the lordship of Christ.

· 6

Repentance and God's Mercy

TO UNDERSTAND more of the marvelous riches of the gospel, we are inevitably led to the biblical teachings on eschatology, the doctrine of "last things." By "eschatology" I do not refer to the various schools of eschatology known as amillenialism, premillenialism and postmillenialism, although what is said has bearing on these positions. Rather, I am talking about the division by the biblical writers of the history of redemption into two main epochs—"in time past" and "these last days" (Heb. 1:1–2).

Now the climactic event of "these last days" is the manifestation of the Lord of glory, Jesus Christ. God has entered into history, and this gives people everywhere a powerful, unprecedented reason for repenting. Let's examine the way Scripture ties the two together.

According to the Bible, the whole of creation and history is designed to glorify God. God is the all-glorious Creator. The first duty of every creature is to praise God for His excellence and give thanks to Him in a spirit of dependent gratitude.

However, the book of Romans teaches us that humanity "knew God," but "did not glorify Him as God, nor were thankful" (Rom. 1:21). Instead, they "changed the glory of the incorruptible God into an image made like corruptible man—and birds and four-footed animals and creeping things" (Rom. 1:23). Thus, to sin is to attack the divine glory—to fight against the person of God and to blind yourself to the Father's goodness in sending rain and sunshine, with fruitful harvests, to rebels who have inverted the Creator-creature relationship and made themselves the object of their own worship.

But God yet seeks to stir thankless hearts to repentance by the gifts of nature and family life (Rom. 2:4; Acts 14:17, 17:25–27). People, however, misinterpret these blessings. They think they are due to them because of their own nobility or misread them as the gift of their idols (Hos. 2:8). Such perversions could only come from a heart that loves to twist reality. In fact, the sinner's whole life is a lie (Rom. 3:7, 13–18).

Hence, humanity's total existence is inglorious. As an image of God, people were made to reflect in an accurate way the splendor of God. But now they live only to praise and honor themselves and the idolatrous creations of their minds and hands. No one is excluded from this condemnation. "All," says the apostle, "have sinned and fall short of the glory of God" (Rom. 3:23).

In these last days human defiance of the divine Glory reaches the flashpoint. It explodes in cold fury in rejection of Jesus Christ, the incarnate Son of God. Here we see that all sin, in its intent and effect, rejects and defies the person and nature of the living God.

So Charles Hodge writes:

> This great sin of rejecting Jesus Christ as a Savior, it must be remembered, is an often and repeated and long continued sin. It is also one which is chargeable not on the openly wicked merely, but upon those whom the world calls moral. They, too, resist the claims of the Son of God; they, too, refuse His love, and reject His offers. It was when all other messengers had failed, the Lord of the vineyard sent His Son to His disobedient servants, saying, "They will reverence my Son" (Matt. 21:37). The guilt of thus rejecting Christ will never be fully appreciated until the day when He shall sit on the throne, and from His face the earth and heaven shall flee away, and no place be found for them.[8]

Nevertheless, even the perceptive Hodge has not fully caught the eschatological seriousness of the sin of unbelief in relationship to Jesus Christ.

Consider for a moment the prologue to the Gospel of John. In the opening verse we learn that "the Word" is God in the fullest sense of the term (John 1:1). Further, this Word was the means by which the Father created the world (John 1:3). And it is this One who entered the world which He had made. John says that *yet* "the world did not know Him" (John 1:10).

This is the ultimate historical crisis. The Author of history has come into space and time and receives wrath and hatred from humanity. John explains, "The Word became flesh and dwelt among us, and we beheld His glory, the glory as of the only begotten of the Father, full of grace and truth" (John 1:14). But "His own did not receive Him" (John 1:11).

As the gift of the Father's love, He is the light of the world. Yet humanity spurns the light which issues from the gift of divine love: "Light has come into the world, and men loved darkness rather than light" (John 3:19).

Jesus says, "I am the bread of life. He who comes to Me shall never hunger, and he who believes in Me shall never thirst" (John 6:35). The next verse emphasizes the scandal. "But I said to you that you have seen Me and *yet* do not believe" (John 6:36). They have seen, but refused to believe— in spite of the very presence of the Son of God whose words and works powerfully testify to the truth of His claims.

What can be done for sinners like these? They are dominated by an iron self-assertion which prefers their own glory to the glory of God (John 5:39–47, 12:41–43). Even more, what can be done for us, since we all participate in that spirit of unbelief which sent the Lord of glory to the cross?

The answer is the cross itself. We have all sinned against the law of God, and now this rebellion has come to climactic expression in our sinning against the ultimate gift of God. But the cross includes in it payment for this worst sin of all—the scorning of it.

This is the wonder of the Father's love. In the new day the crucifixion brings in the hour of glory (John 12:23–24, 31–41, 13:31–32). It represents the noontime brightness of God's infinite compassion. Lifted up, the Son of Man will be made sin so that all who receive Him as the gift of the Father will also enter into glory with Him (John 3:13–16, 17:22).

The work of the Spirit will be concentrated right here. He will, says Jesus, "convict the world of sin." And what is this sin? It is that *they do not believe in Me*" (John 16:8–9).

The cross reveals God's perfect righteousness, and the resurrection vindicates the divine name by establishing Jesus as Victor over sin, death and the devil. In the preaching of the crucifixion and resurrection, people will see and believe in Jesus and enter into eternal life.

But what does this message of glory in John's Gospel have to do with repentance? After all, the word "repentance" does not occur as such in this Gospel.

Nevertheless, this New Testament book helps bring the concept of repentance into the sharpest focus, and at this juncture there are three important truths which need to be firmly nailed down.

First, this teaching makes us realize the depth of our guilt in a new way. Modern humanity does not take unbelief seriously. Often people are even proud of their skepticism about the person and work of Christ. And their more polite indifference to the cross is rarely considered to be tied in with the most fundamental of human sins. Even believers often have a very shallow view of the seriousness of their unbelief in respect to the revelation of the glory of God in the face of Jesus Christ. Unbelief is the supreme transgression of the world—and as your sin too, it is most dangerous to your spiritual life. Specifically, unbelief kills our love and feeds our pride.

Second, a true repentance as distinguished from penance always "flows from the apprehension of the mercy of God." [9] Jesus makes clear that unbelief as the supreme sin is covered over by His sacrifice on Calvary as the supreme gift of the Father's mercy.

In other words, repentance can only be genuine and lasting when evildoers see that God's mercy is available to them.

Put grace in an unreachable realm and you simply deepen the convicted sinner's despair and opposition to God. But John's Gospel banners forth the absolutely finished character of Jesus' work (John 4:34, 17:4, 19:30). There is enough love, and more, accessible to any sinner who wants it. One drop of Jesus' blood will, as it were, atone for the worst of human sins. How then can we fail to respond when we are assured that cleansing love flows in *superabundance* from Calvary?

Jesus then teaches us that repentance for the worst of sins is freely given to believers on the basis of the greatest of gifts. Thus, it is not just the sight of my unbelief that makes me wish to repent, but my seeing the magnitude of the heavenly love.

When the Holy Spirit opened Charles Wesley's heart to this saving knowledge, he struggled to express the wonder of it all in a new song. Note the words:

> And can it be that I should gain
> An interest in the Savior's blood?
> *Died He for me who caused His pain?*
> *For me who Him to death pursued?*
> Amazing love! How can it be
> That Thou my God, shouldst die for me?[10]

Third, from this Gospel you receive a much clearer view of the relationship between faith and repentance.

Our ultimate sin is in our blind unbelief which murders the Son of God. And how do we repent of this sin? By believing in Christ. And how do we believe in Christ? By turning with genuine sorrow from our unbelief and trusting in Christ.

Repentance thus is the more negative side of conversion, the overturning of the idols and the turning to God; saving faith is the more positive side of conversion. As used in Acts, the term "repentance" is comprehensive enough to mean conversion, and it clearly includes trust in Christ alone as Redeemer. As used in John's Gospel, "believing" is an action of the whole person in going to Christ in surrender, a movement which means far more than a superficial acceptance of the facts about Christ's death and resurrection. In this Gospel faith is never used as a noun. It occurs only in verb form and thus signifies a heartfelt appropriation of Christ, a response to the gospel which includes a true hatred of sin as we behold the glory of the crucified Lord.

· 7

Repentance and Counseling

PREVIOUSLY I said that contemporary men and women tend to be *impulse*-ridden. Often they are also deeply *guilt*-ridden. There is a connection. Impulsive, undisciplined people feel guilty because the disordered character of their lives has destroyed the basis for self-respect. They feel inferior for a good reason: They act inferior, perhaps never having completed a task or having done work with their whole heart.

Thus, self-condemnation is an inevitable result of falling below the standard of their own conscience. Distorted by original sin, the conscience yet functions as the authoritative voice of God in the soul (Rom. 2:14–15). This is the constitutive law of humanity, received from the hand of its Maker.

But to evade God's condemnation, people erect about themselves a protective wall of self-righteousness. Adam did it neatly. When the Lord God questioned him about his first disobedience, he put the blame upon his Maker and the woman. Scripture records that "the man said, 'The woman *whom you gave to be with me,* she gave me of the tree, and I ate'" (Gen. 3:12). Note the emphasis. The fault lay with God's gift to the man and only secondarily with the action of the man.

But this self-defense is worthless. A dark restlessness pervades all humanity's inner spaces. No matter how hard people try, they cannot finally escape from this inner torment by moving rapidly through the outer physical spaces—though this is a favorite device adopted by those who live in a self-energized speed culture.

Oh yes, vast multitudes of men and women today officially worship a god who is an innocuous father-figure that they call upon to ease the burden of a restless, self-assertive existence. But in the background a dark cloud of guilt still broods over the troubled waters. Such people's real god is a severe judge who constantly accuses the conscience far more than the father-figure of liberalism or the super-psychiatrist of popular theosophy. So in spite of their religious talk, people today are prone to fear their god in an unhealthy, slavish manner.

A deep blindness has shut their eyes. Because they are under the dominion of darkness (Col. 1:13, Acts 26:18), they think that safety lies in concealment—in the hiding of their sins. They often compare their lives with the lives of other sinners, and on that basis pretend all is well with their souls. Their hearts have never learned that "he who covers his sins will not prosper, but whoever confesses and forsakes them will have mercy" (Prov. 28:13).

What is more, their morbid view of God leads them to suspect that becoming a real Christian would consist of giving up the things they like to do most of all and beginning to do the things they like least.

So there is the barrier. They instinctively think of faith and repentance as human works, as attainments of their own self-effort, when in reality their attempts at confession are rooted in self-assertion. Inevitably, they are left impotent and discouraged. Hence, the problem is how to show them that *they are missing out*, that the joy and peace and glory are all there for those who know the Lord in truth.

To break through the barrier, I have found in counseling sessions that the Gospel of John, the Galatian epistle and Isaiah 53 are not just useful, but *powerfully transforming*. I simply share with troubled people what Christ has done for me through these passages of Scripture, letting them know that if God could renew a sinner like me, He certainly can do the same for others.

Several examples from my life shed light on how God works. The first represents a failure on my part. Some years ago, a depressed young woman came to me for counsel. She was burdened down by a heavy sense of guilt. She was especially troubled over a sexual sin which had been committed about three years prior to this time.

My inability to help stemmed in good part from confusion in my thinking. My assumption was that the gospel was basically for normal people, but that people with psychological problems required a special medical expertise which I lacked. After all, who wants to deepen someone's depression by arousing more feelings of guilt?

It is now clear to me that I was very good at missing the

obvious. In particular, I erred in accepting her Christian profession at face value. At no time did she evidence any fruit of the Spirit, the mind of Christ or a forgiving attitude. In fact, she was guilt-ridden for an excellent reason. She *was* guilty, really and objectively before God. Intensely egocentric, she was morose, spoiled, willful and filled with corrosive self-pity. To top it off, she was bitterly self-righteous and angry at God for not giving her strength to withstand the sexual temptation which had come to her three years before.

In saying this I am not condemning her from a position of self-righteousness. I do not for a moment think such a person is worse than the rest of us. Frankly, the human nature inherited from Adam is pretty nasty stuff, and we ought to expect that the flesh will only produce the deeds of the flesh.

However, I seriously erred by not prayerfully opening the Bible to the fifth chapter of Galatians, where she could compare her life with the works of the flesh produced by the old person to the fruit of the Spirit generated in the life of the new creation (Gal. 5:16–26). If, in spite of all the negative evidence, she was a regenerate person, the Scripture would have brought her to repentance and new life. But— and this is more likely—if she was unconverted, she could have found the joy of salvation through faith in Christ.

The second example: A troubled young man came to me after a worship service. Convinced of the infallibility of Scripture, he had separated from a modernist denomination two years before and was now a Sunday School teacher and trustee in a nearby congregation. In response to my questions about his Christian life, however, he gave answers that were thoroughly legalistic and self-oriented. If his own statements were to be believed, he had no saving knowledge of Christ.

He then blurted out, "I know all the answers you would like to hear, but I have to be honest. What I have told you comes from my heart."

Moved with compassion, I told him, "If your answers have really come from your heart, then you are not yet a Christian."

His face flushed. As he continued to talk, it became even clearer that his knowledge of Christian things was dictionary-oriented. He knew the evangelical vocabulary, but the gospel was only floating on the surface of his consciousness.

Therefore, we opened the Gospel of John to those passages where the sin of unbelief is so powerfully exposed. We read John 1:14, which speaks of Christ as the Word become flesh, the glory of God Incarnate, the overflowing grace. Then we looked at John 1:10, which states that though "the world was made through Him, . . . the world did not know Him." We noted that the spirit of the world is willfully blind, in a deep sense, because it *sees but refuses to believe.* The condemnation is that the light of God's love has dawned in Christ. But people prefer the darkness because their deeds are evil (John 3:18–21).

"This is," I explained, "precisely your guilt, your blindness. Week after week you have heard Christ preached and have closed your heart. You yourself have read and studied the Bible again and again, but you have never tasted of Christ. The Bread of Life has been set before you in all its sufficiency. And you haven't even taken the crumbs."

Then we read John 6:35–36 in which Jesus says, "I am the bread of life. He who comes to Me shall never hunger, and he who believes in Me shall never thirst. But I said to you that *you have seen Me and yet do not believe.*"

"This is the scandal of man's sin," I concluded. "You have sinned not only against the law of God, but you also have sinned against God's love. Yet God is very, very merciful, because the cross will even cover the sin of despising it. This is the work of the Spirit of God. Jesus said, 'When [the Spirit] has come, He will convict the world of sin, . . . because they do not believe in Me' (John 16:8–9)."

The full force of this truth began to reach the young man's heart. When he bowed his head in prayer, he knew the anguish of a repentant Job who cried, "I have heard of You by the hearing of the ear, but now my eye sees You. Therefore I abhor myself, and repent in dust and ashes" (Job 42:5–6). But by the time he had finished his prayer, spontaneous praises poured from his lips. "Thank you, Father! Thank you, thank you, for saving me!" He went from the church building praising God and zealous to witness to the saving power of Christ.

What impresses me is the power of the gospel. No one could have turned this guilt-laden church member into a liberated believer. Only the gospel of God could do that as the Holy Spirit applied it to the heart. I was struck by the harmony between faith and repentance. For believing in Christ—the committal of a soul to the Lord in a faith-surrender—involves a deep humbling that is the same as the contrition of repentance.

In another instance a young couple came to our home for spiritual help. Unknown to us, the wife had been involved with the occult while in college. Exactly how that affected her I am not prepared to say, but she certainly was blinded to the reality of sin and the glory of Christ.

After four hours of discussion, she told me flatly, "I wish

you would show me some of my sins. I really don't know of any." This was very humbling, because that was what I had been trying to do for the whole evening.

But suddenly the Holy Spirit took over in an amazing way. She broke off in the middle of a sentence while mentioning a sin of her husband. "Why," she said, "I think that is my sin too."

Then for a full hour her heart spilled over as she confessed sin after sin to God. There was no question that a sovereign work of Christ's Spirit was taking place. But she could not call God "Father." The words "Holy Father" just could not be formed by her lips.

Awed by this working of God, I interrupted her. "I want to pray," I said. And I confessed my sin of unbelief in not seeing the greatness of Christ's glory and saving power. In doing this I quoted part of John 16:8–9: "He will convict the world of sin, and of righteousness, . . . because they do not believe in Me."

But at this point the young woman said, "That's it! That's it! That's my sin!"

And the next thing I knew, she had taken my prayer from me and was pleading with God to forgive her for her failure to trust in Jesus and for her indifference to the glory of His person.

I do not recall the exact words at this stage of her confession, but I do know that suddenly she could call God "Father." And she called Him Father before she realized what had happened. Then when it dawned upon her what she was doing, praise poured from her lips. How she delighted in the freedom of daughtership as she called God "my Father," "my heavenly Father."

The liberty that followed upon this repentant faith was beautiful beyond description. Soon after, other lives were changed through her spontaneous testimony to the splendor of God's new administration of grace in Christ.

To be sure, not everyone locked into doubt and despair is a non-Christian. Recently, a young minister confessed with tears that his ministry was completely lifeless and that he had no spiritual power whatsoever.

He was directed to the book of Galatians and Isaiah 53. He went away weeping, but after two hours of prayer and reading these parts of the Bible, he returned filled with joy. He said in effect, "I have the joy back again, joy that I had before. So I know I was a Christian before this. My ministry began well. God blessed me a great deal. But I became proud, and then things began going wrong. And before long, all the power disappeared. Then I despaired and began to torture myself with feelings of guilt.

"But when I now encountered Isaiah 53 and Galatians, I saw that I was despising the cross and had fallen into legalistic self-punishment. What a relief to take it all to the cross!" What the man had learned was the difference between legalistic penance and the joys of true repentance and faith.

In another instance a woman was plunged into depression for over two years, apparently with no hope of relief. More than once she had a complete nervous collapse. She had attempted suicide. The psychiatrist and his tools—tranquilizers and shock treatments—had not helped. But the gospel did.

At first she refused to pray with us. "It won't work," she said. "I've tried and it doesn't help."

However, we insisted upon reading Isaiah 53 to her. Again

and again my wife and I came back to one central theme: "You are doing penance for your sins. You are despising the cross of Christ by trying to reenact Calvary in your life as though you were Christ."

Using verses 1–4 of Isaiah 53, we stressed that her guilt was set forth here. She was despising and rejecting Jesus, the "Man of sorrows" (Isa. 53:3).

"But," we added, "here is the great mystery of the love of God. It is too big to take in except by faith. The mystery is that Christ's sacrifice includes in it payment for our despisal and indifference—and you repent of such a sin by trusting in Jesus' blood for cleansing."

Of course, human relationships also had to be set right. But having done this, that night the woman was able to sleep normally for the first time in months, and within a short time she returned to a full work schedule. Back in church, she now gives God full credit for what He alone has done by the power of His Spirit. She says that she could not have imagined that God could so swiftly revive and restore to her the Christian joy which had been formerly hers.

Her experience is worth further reflection. It points up the danger which constantly faces both new believers and long-time Christians. It is the temptation to think of the first conversion as everything and to forget that repentance and faith include a continuing, radical reorientation of the life toward God. Hear what John Murray says: "Christ's blood is the laver of initial cleansing but it is also the fountain to which the believer must continuously repair. It is at the cross of Christ that repentance has its beginning; it is at the cross of Christ that it must continue to pour out its heart in the tears of confession and contrition."[11]

In the words of the apostle Paul, it means that people "should repent, turn to God, and *do works befitting repentance*" (Acts 26:20). Repentant believers have the power to perform the deeds of repentance because they are in life-union with the resurrected Christ. They are full of the Holy Spirit and through earnest prayer seek and receive more of the fullness of God from the Father (Luke 11:5–13). They are no victims of impersonal forces, either physiological or spiritual. They are Christ's free creation.

But the standing temptation is for believers to allow their lives to fill up with sins and to slip back into the old habit of self-assertion and self-trust. When this happens, their "repentings" often lose their power because self-trust has led them to legalistic ground as a basis for their acceptance with God. Without faith in Christ, repentance becomes soul-chilling remorse.

To keep this from happening, representatives of the gospel must do their work faithfully. Christ, "the Lion of the tribe of Judah, . . . has prevailed to open the scroll and to loose its seven seals" (Rev. 5:5). He has done His work and done it well. Now, by the energy which He mightily inspires in us, let us do ours. Our work is to teach and preach the gospel in a searching manner, to lay the basis for repentance by showing sinners how much they need the Lord of glory as Savior from their guilt and filth. It is a solemn fact that God has ordained that men and women be saved through preaching.

But today many hold back part of the truth through ignorance, or they state the truth abstractly and narrowly, or even fail to give the gospel the cutting edge of specific application. This means that sinners are being robbed of the opportunity to repent because of a message that is dulled by pride and self-dependence.

What is needed, therefore, is a humbling among the bearers of the gospel. At present, complacency is the biggest single stumbling block to the ministry of the Spirit. The need of the hour is for bold, loving preaching by those on fire for the glory of Christ, people of prayer who will not rest until the Lord establishes Jerusalem as a praise in the earth (Isa. 62:6–7).

Effective counseling is principally a carrying forward in private of specific applications of the preaching ministry in the church. The gospel message is announced boldly in a public context, then given added effectiveness by a one-to-one follow-up in dealing with particular idols which Christ wants removed from each of our lives. Such confrontation in preaching and counseling involves a sensitivity to the heart cries of men and women. It combines tears and truth as we bow together before the discipline of God's Word.

The warfare here is spiritual and calls for great courage on the part of God's ambassadors.

Courage!

Courage to ask yourself if you are lulling people to sleep by a message that fosters self-congratulation rather than repentance to life.

Courage first to teach your own heart and then to teach others that there are only two ways to stand before God: either as a contrite publican or a self-righteous Pharisee (Luke 18:9–14).

It will not be easy to tell those outside of Christ that their lives are built on *presumption* and *pretense*. And it will not be easy to tell confessing Christians that they too have taken for granted God's blessings upon their lives.

Symptoms of this are vividly demonstrated in the modern home. At present things are profoundly wrong. With the current increase of divorces, the time may not be far off when in some areas divorces per month may equal the number of marriages.

Many homes are distorted by husbands who refuse to take positive, loving leadership! And over against these soft-boned men stand self-assertive wives who want their own way—sometimes at any cost.

Add to this the sham of a double standard. Who has the spiritual fortitude to tell parents in plain terms that mouth-righteousness without heart-righteousness will drive their children away from the things of God?

Roles and rules are confused. Lines of authority are undefined. Inevitably, children arrive at mature years unequipped for adulthood. Having been given too much, they are spoiled, selfish and willful. This is not true of everyone, of course, but these trends are so widespread that they are really epidemic.

Strangely enough, the permissiveness of a John Dewey and a Dr. Benjamin Spock has not led to liberation. Instead, the removal of the boundaries of law has led to a sense of unlimited guilt, with many young people openly confessing that they feel about as valuable as trash. The reason for this self-despisal is that the parents make powerful and unspoken demands upon their children without realizing the inability of their children to fulfill them. Often these unexpressed standards are impossibly high and unrealistic. Parents rarely know how to deal honestly with their own sins, not to mention those of their children.

Through our union with Christ established by faith, we

have the power to reorient our lives so that forgiving and forgetting can prevail in the home. Freedom can come to the home through a return to God's order for the family, which means respect and dignity for the headship of the husband.

Christian husbands, God gives you an urgent message—the message of repentance to life. Has your heart been crushed by the knowledge of your failure to train your family in the principles of the Word of God? Have you taught your children the joys of daily repentance through heart-searching prayer?

But these symptoms of presumption and pretense are not limited to the home. They can be found in the congregation of those who claim to uphold the orthodoxy of the Reformation and fundamentalist standards.

Pastor, how many officers in your church live only on the resources of a past Christian experience whose fires have long ago gone out? How many separated saints have allowed the joints of the gospel armor to rust together through secret pride? And what about the churches which have become gossip centers without anyone honestly facing up to the fact?

But, preacher, you have the answer.

People are oppressed by the law of sin and death. They are oppressed by guilty consciences and the prospect of divine judgment. However, *you* have the gospel message which can change all of this. From it sinners learn of a bleeding sacrifice which does what the law of sin and death could never do. It brings expiation for sins and the washing of the conscience through a new dominion established by Jesus' resurrection.

In this message Christ, the risen Lord, is set forth in all His glory (2 Cor. 3:18). He can do what no mere human counseling can do. By turning to the Lord, i.e., by repenting, individuals can come into possession of this divine splendor revealed in Christ (2 Cor. 3:16–18).

Since saving power comes from Christ alone, it has seemed increasingly important to me of late to emphasize to those under conviction of sin that they retire and pray privately in coming to Christ. My reasons for this are twofold: First, prayer in private makes it more difficult for people to use the counselor as a priest and hopefully brings them to rely on Christ alone for salvation; and second, prayer alone brings the glory of Christ into sharp focus by moving the counselor out of the sinner's line of vision.

Later, when repentant sinners recall their turning to Christ, they will have things on a solid basis. They will find their confidence in Christ and the gospel, not in the presence or absence of another person, and spontaneously they will give the Lord of glory credit for what He has done through the gospel message.

The gospel message is a mirror in which all repentant sinners behold the image of Christ and are being transformed from glory to glory through the power of the Spirit.

Do not underestimate it. For the gospel enables those who are new creations to face their own sins squarely, confess them and forsake them.

Do not underestimate it. For the gospel brings forgiveness to us through Christ's death.

Repentance and Sharing Christ

UNTIL we have experienced the breaking down of pride by the Holy Spirit, we do not understand what witnessing is all about.

We may think we do. We may even give our "testimony." More likely we shall prefer the line of thought which hands witnessing responsibility over to the ministers. In some instances pastors will even take this a step further and hand the task over to those ministers "with a special evangelistic gift."

What is the problem? At bottom it is that many confessing Christians think they are too weak to witness. They say, "If I knew the Bible better, or if I were a stronger Christian, then I would witness."

But in reality they are too strong to witness. Not strong in the Lord, of course, but strong in themselves. Naturally, they have a concern to protect themselves from the world, and they do a good job of it. In fact, they protect themselves by never really getting involved with sinners.

However, when you are weak in the Pauline sense, you are both painfully and joyfully aware of your need for Christ. Being empty, you have room for the fullness of Christ as Savior, Lord, Priest and Teacher. You sense that you don't even know how to pray, at least not honestly in the presence of God. Unless Christ by His Spirit continually searches you out, you see your life almost immediately clogged with indifference, self-will, envy, pride, lust and unbelief. You know that yesterday's love to God can be swiftly washed away by today's fear and worry.

But such a knowledge of your heart will not be the cause of a spiritual defeat. On the contrary, the awareness of great weakness paves the way for a thoroughgoing repentance that results in a filling with the Holy Spirit's power. Your conviction of sin is used by the Lord to bring you to claim the victory of grace in Him.

Satan, on the other hand, would much prefer to cloak such self-awareness with a spirit of blindness. It may serve his interests to make you very religious, but his strategy is always to make you only half a sinner and give you only half a Christ.

The Deceiver may serve up a "Jesus" who is a wise teacher, a Jewish Socrates who is yet greater than Socrates because he teaches about the universal Fatherhood of God. He may entice you to worship the "martyred Jesus." He may seduce you into putting your faith in the creed rather than in the Jesus who is so admirably described in the creed. Or if you are alert to all these dangers, he may prompt you to worship in your mind an image of Christ derived from an artist's head of Christ or from distorted childhood recollections of Jesus which came to you through Sunday School art.

Again, it may be in the devil's interests to get you to stop praying altogether. But often his greatest successes come when he can get you to pray with amazing fluency—especially for the benefit of your own emotional consolation or for your hearers.

These wiles of Satan are countered by honesty in prayer. Honest prayer unmasks your real need and puts you in the presence of a rich Christ who wants to meet you as you really are—"wretched, miserable, poor, blind, and naked" (Rev. 3:17).

It can be a struggle even to name your sin before God. You flounder because the name you give your sin often expresses further evasion.

You pray, "Lord, forgive me for not loving Mrs. X." But in your heart you can still see the obnoxious image of Mrs. X, and the vision does not exactly attract your compassion. And the sentimentalized image of Jesus which floats through your consciousness has no power to banish your evil thoughts about this woman.

Then the Jesus at the Father's right hand begins to do His sovereign work. Suddenly you realize through the Holy Spirit that you have been trifling. Now you pray differently, with a stricken conscience, "Holy Father, I have not loved Mrs. X. But that's only part of my sin. In my heart I have despised her."

So in your confession to God you fight to name your sin—*and to give your sin its right name.* Then you hand it over to Christ by faith and taste the happiness of guilt forgiven (Ps. 32:1) and find the deliverance from hypocrisy which comes through honest confession (Ps. 32:2–5).

What you now know is almost beyond words, but has

the feel of clear shining after rain, sunshine after tears. Grace is for sinners, and you have felt grace make a clean sweep of your repentant heart. God loves you where you are, not where you have been pretending to be. There is a natural transition now to start loving other sinners where they are, not where they pretend to be—or where you think they should be.

So to use an expression coined by Bill Milliken in his book *Tough Love,* "little conversions" must happen many times to the Christian after the first turning to the Lord. In these life-and-death battles, you begin to understand that you personally must have your dirty feet washed daily by Jesus and that you need daily to get down on your knees and wash the feet of the other disciples.

In the twentieth century, Christians ran into great difficulty in effectively communicating the gospel to the world, except perhaps for a limited part of the Protestant middle class. The modern world, to be sure, has been powerfully opposed to the gospel. Scientific rationalism has poisoned the minds of people against supernatural Christianity, and sensualism and materialism have seduced their hearts. Postmodern thinking today continues to undermine the gospel message. Yet hostility to the things of God was at least equally evident in the first, sixteenth and eighteenth centuries, but God worked powerfully in those times. So the enmity of the world is not the basic cause of contemporary powerlessness in witnessing.

The core problem is that we are inviting men and women to come under the power of the gospel without having first come under its power ourselves. Frankly, I know of very few confessing Christians who have ever shed tears over their sins. Or if once they wept over their sins, they are careful never to do it again; they see no one else doing it, and they quickly become convinced that people who shed tears are not normal Christians.

We feel that it is more Christian to remain aloof, to be *tough*. We may believe that it is proper to run roughshod over the Spirit's gentle entreaties while we worry and work, convinced that we are strong enough to make it by ourselves with only an occasional assist from God. The last thing we want to admit is that we are weak, foolish and sinful. But we are tense in our imagined righteousness.

What we really need is just to face the truth about ourselves. When we do that, our lives have a special appeal to God and to unbelievers. God loves to hear a person cry out in heartbroken honesty, "Lord, I am nothing but a poor sinner. Send help quickly or I'll die!"

But what has this to do with witness? Everything!

God loves such a spirit (Luke 18:9–14). And not surprisingly, other sinners are instinctively drawn to the contrite Christian. They do not know exactly what it is about the humbled believer that attracts them, but they retain something of an awareness of God's being and workings (Rom. 1:18–23, 32, 2:14–15). They can sense the presence of God when Christians surrender their hearts to the Father—including their self-tainted virtues, skills and knowledge.

Humility and sincere love appeal in any age. But in ours these qualities become especially magnetic. On the one hand, these things are in very short supply. And on the other, in the current era sinners have attempted the overthrow of every absolute except one. That absolute is *compassion joined with integrity.*

Clear-eyed compassion! Most moderns at least give lip-service to this as the last universal, the only firm centerpiece in a disintegrating world.

But here's the pinch. There is nothing left for our contemporaries to hang the centerpiece on. Openness, caring and simple honesty are rapidly disappearing from the contemporary scene. Ours is the plight of the "ragged urchin" in W. H. Auden's "The Shield of Achilles":

> That girls are raped, that two boys knife
>   a third,
> Were axioms, to him who'd never heard
>   of any world where promises were kept,
> Or one could weep because another wept.[12]

Nevertheless, modern humanity does not need to despair. For the union of compassion and integrity is to be found in the one who repents. These things are the fruits of repentance. People with broken and contrite hearts have learned something about love and honesty before God. No longer are they crusaders driven by a proud human emptiness.

True, as they grow in holiness, they sense the acute difference between themselves and the world. They take seriously sin and Satan, and by the authority of the cross, they reckon themselves dead to the power of darkness. For that reason they cannot accept a one-world theology which emphasizes the solidarity of all people as one spiritual race. Unrepentant sinners are still in darkness. The repentant are now in God's kingdom.

But repentant people also know that they have a great deal in common with all humanity. Although they have been cleansed by the precious blood of Christ, they are still human, and they are also sinners. As their repentance deepens they learn to see other people compassionately. They know that God broke through their own thick shell, and that all good in themselves originated with a sovereign invasion from without. It is therefore most natural for them to feel mercy for others as they drink from the overflowing Spirit of Christ. They touch peoples' sins and sicknesses with the fingers of their hearts.

This humbled spirit embodies the essence of Christianity. It gives all the glory to the Father in the name of the Son through the power of the Holy Spirit. Salvation is altogether the free gift of the triune God. God is seen to be *infinitely majestic* and yet also *infinitely personal* as He binds Himself in a covenant of love to unworthy sinners.

Hence, if the faith is genuine, it results in believers deepening their humanity and their sympathetic concern for others in their peril of eternal judgment.

But a religion without deep love to God and compassion for the lost is a contradiction in terms, a monstrosity which is unworthy of the name "Christian." It may well prove to be nothing but cold, unrepentant deism disguising itself under the noble banner of orthodoxy.

So the aim of it all is to get a loving integrity which comes only from a life lived in the presence of God. It is this kind of life which energizes believers to witness and gives the testimony great power. Therefore, whatever particular strategy you may use in the work, remember—practically everything hinges on your loving boldness in presenting the gospel (Eph. 6:18–20, 1 Thess. 1:5).

But where do you get this spirit of loving freedom in witness? You have already seen the answer in the beginning of this chapter on repentance and witnessing: It comes through prayer.

Yet it is one thing to be told something and another to believe it—to take the matter seriously.

Listen and obey.

You find witnessing power only by going to the throne of grace and coming to Christ to get yourself clean and under the blessing of God. From there you go forth to share what you have received firsthand from the Father.

This is the beating heart of Christian witness. In evangelism everything depends upon a humble, self-forgetting boldness before God and humanity. *Pray boldly and you will witness boldly* (Eph. 6:18–20, 1 Thess. 1:5, Acts 4:29–31). Confess your sins freely before God, and you will have freedom to confess Christ before others.

Some churches have almost nothing in the way of converts because they stand on a pedestal of formalism when they pray. We ask for very little and consequently receive very little (James 4:2). Furthermore, when we do pray fervently for boldness, we forget that God gave us feet. Feet carry the gospel; lips must proclaim it. Paul's question is still relevant: "How shall they hear without a preacher?" (Rom. 10:14).

Do you wish to maintain your dignity at all costs? Are you afraid to get the gospel into the world's marketplaces? Friend, consider the cross, God's way of salvation. Was there dignity in that? Of course not. And you too must go the way of the cross, crucifying pride and timidity. The people of the world slandered George Whitefield, stoned Henry Martyn and threw cow dung on W. C. Burns. Why should you be an exception?

John Calvin says, "Fear hinders us from preaching Christ openly and fearlessly, while the absence of all restraint and disguise in confessing Christ is demanded from His ministers."[13] The remedy for this timidity is to carry the sin directly to God in prayer until He fills the penitent heart with an ongoing love that refuses to be stopped by the resistance of sinners to the gospel.

Isn't it about time that you, my fellow reader, became indignant over your policy of drift and easy compromise?

Come now, let us clear ourselves from all the rubbish of sin that we have allowed to collect in our lives. Then when the Lord calls us to share the good news with the lost, we will be able to say in good conscience with a repentant Isaiah, "Here am I! Send me" (Isa. 6:8).

Epilogue

It was a beautiful day in Cuernavaca, Mexico, a small resort town sixty miles south of Mexico City. The sun was warm; the sky was a clear bright blue; the pink azaleas were in full bloom; and the purple bougainvillea cast its reflection on the pool. This was the peaceful scene my husband Jack and I saw from the balcony of our room at Chula Vista, the Alpha-Omega Center for Missionary Outreach where Jack was speaking at a conference.

But inside our room the scene was anything but peaceful. Our eighteen-year-old daughter Barbara had just announced that she did not want anything to do with our rules, our way of life or our faith. She didn't want any restraints—not from us or from God. She announced, "I'm not a Christian, and I don't want to fake it anymore."

We didn't know what to say. I tried yelling, but of course that didn't work. Barbara just yelled back. Jack just listened quietly to both of us. Later he said to me, "I need to understand God's love in a deeper way." He spent the next two weeks writing about God's love and how it is experienced through repentance. He realized that he couldn't mend our broken relationship with Barbara, but he could learn to depend on his heavenly Father—the only One who can change sinners. So he wrote about the joy that comes from humbling ourselves before God in repentance and faith. He wrote *Repentance* to remind himself and me that we were no different than Barbara—just helpless sinners who needed to turn from our sins and toward our heavenly Father who welcomes us for Jesus' sake.

After we returned to Philadelphia, there were many times that Jack was tempted to be filled with anger and despair as Barbara went her own way. Again and again he had to go back to the truths he had written and ask God to cleanse him from the sins he saw displayed in his relationship with Barbara: pride, wanting to be in control and unbelief. As Barbara's life went from bad to worse, he kept returning to his need for the presence of the Spirit, which God gives to the humble and contrite.

When others came to him for help, he often handed them the unpublished manuscript of this small book. We watched as the Spirit of God used it to bring the joy of repentance and humility to many others. In 1973 Jack started New Life Presbyterian Church in the living room of our home. He kept passing out the unprinted book and preaching that repentance is a return to God as the center of all of life. This teaching became the heartbeat of our church. In 1975, three years after *Repentance* was written, Christian Literature Crusade (now CLC Publications) published it as *Repentance and 20th Century Man.*

Jack never separated repentance from the call to carry the gospel to the nations. In *Repentance* he wrote, "You find witnessing power only by going to the throne of grace and coming to Christ to get yourself clean and under the blessing of God. From there you go forth to share what you have received firsthand from the Father. This is the beating heart of Christian witness. . . . everything depends upon a humble, self-forgetting boldness before God and humanity" (p. 90).

While Jack pastored New Life Presbyterian Church, he lived out this teaching by taking the good news of repentance and forgiveness of sins to our next door neighbors, homeless drug addicts and the mentally ill, and then overseas to Europe and Africa. New Life's first mission trip was to Ireland, and two years later Jack brought a team to Uganda after the dictator Idi Amin was driven out of the country.

Jack's life of daily repentance and taking the gospel to some of the hardest places in the world eventually caught the attention of Barbara and her husband Angelo. God worked in their life, and they too stepped into the joy of living in fellowship with God through repentance and faith.

As New Life's mission work continued to expand, Jack began to partner with other churches. In 1983 Jack and our son Paul joined with those churches to start World Harvest Mission, an organization whose purpose is to advance the kingdom of God through bringing to the nations the good news of repentance and forgiveness of sins. As part of their mission, Jack and Paul developed the Sonship Course, a leadership training program that emphasized the love of God and a life characterized by faith and repentance. World Harvest Mission now has 144 missionaries serving in twelve countries, and the Sonship Course has been taught all over the world.

As New Life Church and World Harvest Mission grew, and other churches were planted both in the United States and abroad, Jack kept sharing about the importance of repentance in his preaching, his writing[14] and in the letters he wrote to church planters, leaders and missionaries. He knew how much he struggled with pride and self-importance, and he saw this as a central temptation, especially for those in full-time ministry. When he wrote to a pastor friend, he shared his own continuing struggle with pride and said, "I would like to tell you, Doug, that I have solved this problem once and for all, but this is a struggle that is intense, like tearing the flesh off your bones."[15]

Jack never stopped needing to repent. He knew he needed daily grace from God, and that grace flows to the humble (James 4:6). To him repentance was humility in action—a humility that doesn't stand on the mountain of pride, but instead asks for daily help from the God who gives grace freely to all who ask.

Jack saw his severe health problems as one more opportunity to repent daily and receive the grace that God gives to those who acknowledge their own helplessness. After he survived a severe heart attack in Uganda in 1983 and the onset of lymphoma in 1987, he wrote to a team of missionaries working in Ireland, "Please don't be afraid of the working of God. He calls us to repentance, but in that call supplies the Spirit to bring us to the cleansing of the Lamb. There is no greater joy than leaving our idols at the cross and walking away freed of these cruel bondages. Expect, welcome and treasure repentance in yourselves and others. Let Christ break down sloth, lusts, pride, coldness of heart, prejudices, despair. He has had a great deal of experience cleansing His temples, and you can trust Him to overturn in order to fill you with songs of gladness."[16]

In the early spring of 1996, Jack preached on the glory of God at a church in Germany. He was experiencing chest pains and weakness, but as he spoke about God's glory being on display in the cross of Christ, he was filled with joy. He had learned through many trials to distrust every impulse of his heart and to know the relief that comes when real sins are brought to a real Savior. He was living out what he had written many years before in *Repentance*: "The glory of the cross appeared before my eyes with transforming and healing power" (p. 11). This was the theme of his messages and his life. A few months later, on April 8, 1996, Jack died in Spain after open heart surgery. Now he sees with his own eyes the glory of God.

As I reread this book, I again found that repentance clears the air, gets the heart right with God and gives courage to continue on the path of life. Some of the language is old fashioned, but the central thought that repentance brings us into fellowship with God—and "to be near God and to have God near us is the whole purpose of human life" (p. 12)—is timeless.

As an eighty-three year old widow ministering in London to South Asian women, I see my need to remember this truth and live it out every day. In my teaching, mentoring and developing of friendships, there is always room to repent of lack of compassion, dullness of heart and a self-centered outlook on life. I continually see how much I need to repent and surrender my life and plans to my sovereign Lord Jesus. When I do this, the grace of God flows into my life. As Jack used to say, "Grace flows downhill." Joy always comes to me as I take the lowest place and look to Jesus for forgiveness and grace. My hope and prayer is that God will continue to use this small book to teach the joy of repentance, humility and a life lived in service to our faithful Savior, Jesus Christ.

Rose Marie Miller, May 2008

Endnotes

1. Mark Twain, *The Autobiography of Mark Twain*, Charles Neider, ed. (New York: Harper & Brothers, 1959), p. 42.
2. Ibid., p. 41.
3. Geerhardus Vos, *The Kingdom of God and the Church* (Grand Rapids: Eerdmans, 1951), p. 92.
4. B. B. Warfield, *Biblical and Theological Studies* (Phillipsburg, NJ: P&R Publishing, 1952), p. 363.
5. Lewis Sperry Chafer, *Systematic Theology*, Vol. 3 (Dallas: Dallas Seminary Press, 1948), p. 372.
6. John Colquhoun, *Repentance* (London: Banner of Truth, 1965), p. 32.
7. G. Campbell Morgan, *Evangelism* (Grand Rapids: Baker, 1976), p. 7.
8. Charles Hodge, *The Way of Life* (Carlisle, PA: Banner of Truth, 1978), p. 57.
9. Ibid., p. l61.
10. Charles Wesley, "And Can It Be That I Should Gain" (hymn), 1738.
11. John Murray, *Redemption Accomplished and Applied* (Grand Rapids: Eerdmans, 1955), p. 143.
12. W. H. Auden, "The Shield of Achilles" in *Selected Poetry of W. H. Auden* (New York: Random House, 1958), p. 135.
13. John Calvin, *Commentary on the Epistles of Paul to the Galatians and Ephesians* (Grand Rapids: Eerdmans, 1948), p. 342.
14. Jack also wrote *Powerful Evangelism for the Powerless, Outgrowing the Ingrown Church,* and *Come Back, Barbara. A Faith Worth Sharing* and *The Heart of a Servant Leader: Letters from Jack Miller*, also written by Jack, were published posthumously.
15. *The Heart of a Servant Leader: Letters from Jack Miller.* (Phillipsburg, NJ: P&R Publishing, 2004), p. 57.
16. Ibid., p. 63.

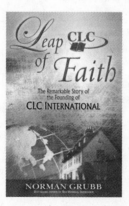

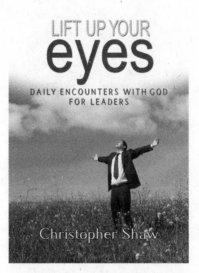

LIFT UP YOUR EYES

Christopher Shaw

Leaders often work under heavy pressure. While the demands of ministry can threaten to overwhelm us, *Lift Up Your Eyes* reminds leaders of the need to focus on the Lord for daily strength.

The kind of life we live when no one is watching will significantly impact our public ministry, but the private lives of most leaders suffer neglect as they try to grow the church. This book emphasizes that our relationship with Christ is our most powerful leadership tool.

Trade paper • 378 pages
978-0-87508-989-8

CLC'S #1 BEST SELLER

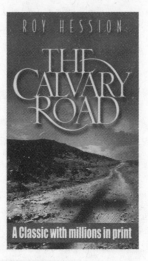

THE CALVARY ROAD

Roy Hession

Do you long for revival and power in your life?

Learn how Jesus can fill you with His Spirit
through brokenness, repentance and confession.

"This is one of the books that made the greatest impact on me as a
young Christian and in the work of Operation Mobilization around
the world. We felt the message of this book was so important that it has
been required reading for all who unite with us.

"I would recommend every believer to read this book, and to follow
up on it by reading *We Would See Jesus*."

George Verwer, Operation Mobilization

Trade paper • 108 pages
978-0-87508-788-4
Mass market • 131 pages
978-0-87508-236-3

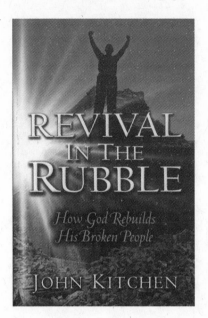

REVIVAL IN THE RUBBLE

John Kitchen

When God wants to do a fresh, reviving work in His people, He finds a person and breaks his heart. John Kitchen uses the book of Nehemiah to show how we can find spiritual renewal out of brokenness.

Trade paper • 261 pages
978-0-87508-873-2

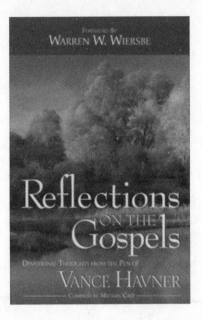

REFLECTIONS ON THE GOSPELS
Vance Havner

Rescued by Michael Catt from a collection of newspaper columns and compiled for the first time in book form, this wonderful devotional gives a unique insight into God's Word through the eyes of a great preacher.

Useful as a personal devotional or as a study tool, this book provides an enlightening and inspiring opportunity to spend a few moments with a New Testament prophet.

Trade paper • 227 pages
978-0-87508-783-3

Best-selling Author of *The Hiding Place*

CORRIE TEN BOOM

with Jamie Buckingham

Join Corrie
on a world-wide journey
that could only
have been planned
by God

T R A M P
FOR THE
LORD

The Story that Begins Where The Hiding Place Ends

TRAMP FOR THE LORD

Corrie ten Boom

This is Corrie ten Boom's story of two decades as a self-styled "tramp for the Lord," as she traveled across the globe, sharing the reality of Jesus Christ. Communicating her experience as a prisoner in a Nazi concentration camp, Corrie tells of God's guidance, forgiveness and power and how she was challenged after her release to live fully the truths she had learned.

Trade paper • 212 pages
978-0-87508-986-7

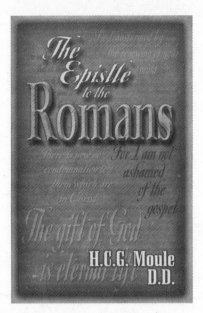

THE EPISTLE TO THE ROMANS
H.C.G. Moule

"In my personal library, there are over sixty volumes on the Epistle to the Romans, and all of them have helped me in one way or another. But for solid theology and spiritual insight, presented in a clear and concise style, none surpasses this volume by Bishop Handley Moule. He knows his Bible, he knew his Greek, he knew his Lord, and he knew how to instruct God's people. I rejoice that this book is again available to a new generation of serious Bible students."

Warren W. Wiersbe
Author and Conference Speaker

Trade paper • 345 pages
978-0-87508-709-4